# FINANCIAL FREEDOM

## How to Profit From Your Perfect Business

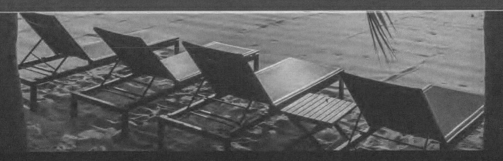

From The International Best Selling Authors

**Dr. Denis Cauvier  &  Alan Lysaght**

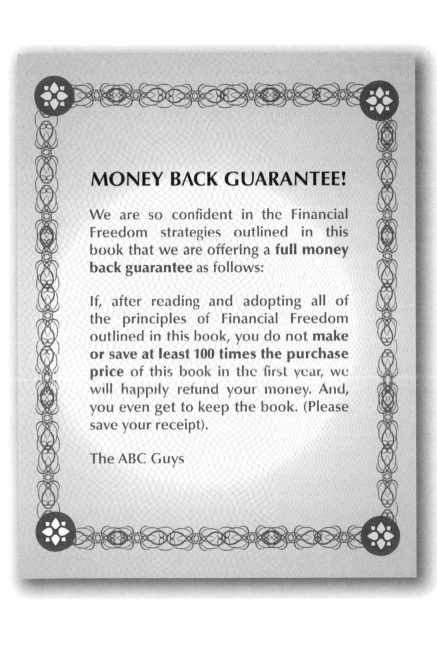

# MONEY BACK GUARANTEE!

We are so confident in the Financial Freedom strategies outlined in this book that we are offering a **full money back guarantee** as follows:

If, after reading and adopting all of the principles of Financial Freedom outlined in this book, you do not **make or save at least 100 times the purchase price** of this book in the first year, we will happily refund your money. And, you even get to keep the book. (Please save your receipt).

The ABC Guys

# Table of Contents

# Financial Freedom

## Introduction

> " 66% of American adults want to own a business, but most either don't know what opportunity to pursue or what is the best way to start.
>
> The Economist "

Financial Freedom. Everyone wants it - it's a no-brainer. Unfortunately, few win the genetic lottery of being born into wealth, meaning that most of us will have to earn our way into it, and that usually means getting a job.

Who wouldn't want to ditch their domineering boss; the colleagues that use the workplace to vent their home life frustrations; the daily grind of work and the restricted freedom, to say nothing of the severe limits on their earning potential? And, after all, who would make a better boss than, well, you? Who would be fairer to the employees; who would be better at making business decisions, and who would be more deserving of the profits? In fact, research tells us even though more than two thirds of Americans want to be business owners, very few take the plunge. For some, there are good reasons for such hesitancy. Our job in this book is to eliminate those reasons one by one.

So, why aren't more people business owners? Much of what holds us back is our Attitude towards business. We call it "the fears between the ears," and it's the cornerstone of our ABCs philosophy, which runs through all of our books and workshops. This philosophy has influenced and helped literally millions of people worldwide, mostly because we break challenges down into simple steps that are easy to achieve. Part of what holds us back is that we have been programmed since childhood that work is something that happens from 9 to 5, with weekends off and several weeks paid vacation. In 2017, this concept has broken down, but people have been so conditioned that anything that doesn't fit this model is automatically rejected. There are definitely other obstacles to business ownership besides self-limiting beliefs. Some of the major non-attitudinal issues include not knowing the right business to pursue, not having enough capital, having a limited skill set, not having a relationship with business coaches or advisors such as lawyers and accountants, and so on. And, in 2017, we have to consider the disrupters. We have entered into the "gig" economy, and the foundations are shifting under the feet of traditional businesses throughout the world.

The good news is that all of these issues can be overcome. Whether you are a high school student considering your options, a recent college graduate, or a sixty-five-year-old looking for a new challenge or a supplement to your retirement income, this book will show you the path to Financial Freedom. Although a huge number of people end up achieving less in life than they were capable of, the very fact that you have picked up this book is a positive statement that you are open to making changes. Over the years we have interviewed and worked with hundreds of self-made millionaires, people who have created at least one successful business. We learned what they do differently – how they think, how they react to challenges, and what sets them apart from the rest of the workforce. There are many things to learn from them, and they're all in this book. Just applying two or three of these strategies will improve your chances for success. But please: don't stop there. Read the whole book. It won't take you long. The more issues you prepare for, the better your chances of success. We really don't want you to invest your time, money or reputation into a project only to be tripped up by something you had overlooked. Financial Freedom is possible for you and your family. Read on.

## Universal Truths:

All of our research and experience has verified the following principles:

- People achieve their dreams when they take control of their lives.
- Education comes in many forms besides college degrees.
- You're never too young or old to become financially free.
- Real opportunities are open to all genders, ages, and races.
- Financial Freedom is possible for average and ordinary people.
- You can fast-track success by tapping into powerful coaches.
- You don't have to inherit or win money to become financially free.
- Anyone can be an entrepreneur.
- For every person there is a perfect business.
- One's past does not necessarily determine their future.
- Some businesses have a much greater chance of success than others.
- Obstacles and adversity provide opportunities for growth.

# Financial Freedom

## Section One: Attitudes That Create Financial Freedom

> **The worst liability in achieving Financial Freedom is having the wrong Attitude. Fortunately it is 100% curable.**
>
> ABC Guys

For many, working for someone else makes perfect sense. You agree to perform a specific task, from answering phones to driving a forklift to selling goods at retail. Your boss is responsible for everything else – from paying all the overhead costs (rent, heat, electricity, etc.) to organizing the marketing and sales departments. The boss also deals with such headaches as covering for sick employees, working around mechanical breakdowns, negotiating with greedy landlords, and calling in the geeks when the website crashes. It's not your concern. So long as you do your job, you get paid. Sometimes weekly, and sometimes, very weakly.

So, why mess with the formula? Why look for responsibility? Well, some people don't like being forced to work within arbitrary time constraints: they hate being scolded, or even fired, for arriving five minutes late because of a tie-up on the freeway. Others resent being told what to wear or what not to wear. Still others chafe at being forced to beg for a raise, which, even if granted, will be largely eaten up by taxes. These are the people that dread Mondays and live for Fridays. But here's the most important thing to remember: it's the business owner, the one who successfully deals with these issues and hires the right people to solve these challenges, who reaps the lion's share of the rewards.

# Hate Your Job?

According to Forbes here are 10 reasons why people hate their jobs. Do any of these sound familiar?

1. They are not respected as people and are viewed only as production units.

2. They don't have the right tools, equipment, information, or other basic requirements for doing their job.

3. Their employer disregards their personal life and has no compassion for their outside obligations.

4. Their immediate supervisor is tyrannical, incompetent, or both.

5. They are tired of being lied to.

6. They have been given no vision of the future.

7. They are tired of dealing with workplace politics.

8. They are underpaid and overworked while the owners keep all of the profits.

9. They feel like they're pushing a rock up a hill and are tired of getting no forward motion.

10. They have to watch every word they say, because they could get in trouble - or fired - for almost any reason.

## An Entrepreneurial Economy

Entrepreneurs hire people and services, purchase raw materials and machinery, and build or lease new offices, warehouses and retail spaces. All of this involves risk, for which they are rewarded by keeping all the net profits AND paying less in taxes. Whereas the average worker has a limited number of tax deductions, entrepreneurs get to deduct any costs associated with building and running their businesses. So if, for example, you sell women's fashions and need to go to Paris and Milan every year to make purchases for the upcoming season, all business related travel expenses come out of the company's pocket, not yours. Nice.

## DID YOU KNOW

Entrepreneurs are the key to any growing economy.

- There are about 24.5 million full and part-time home-based businesses in the United States.

- Nearly 750,000 tax-paying, employee-hiring businesses are started every year.

- Small businesses create 75 percent of the new jobs in the United States.

# Ownership Benefits

According to Inc., these are the most important benefits of having your own business:

1. You control your own destiny because you set the goals, make the decisions, and allocate the resources.

2. You set your own work schedule and pick your own workplace.

3. You select the people you want to work with (partners, employees, or suppliers).

4. You decide which risks to take, and you keep all the rewards for doing so.

5. You can enjoy learning new things and experiencing new opportunities on a daily basis.

6. You can immerse yourself in enjoyable work that you are passionate about.

7. You live a better lifestyle AND get to deduct the costs of your mobile, gas, trips, meals etc.

8. You can build win/win, long-term relationships with your clients and suppliers.

9. You can support your favorite causes because of additional resources and money.

10. You create goodwill that can be sold for a premium, or passed on to your loved ones.

# Financial Freedom

Another nice feature of being the owner is that there are no longer any limits on how much money you make - Not that this is the only reason to own a business. Satisfaction, accomplishment, and succeeding at new challenges are just a few of the others - So let's say you are the manager of a retail outlet and you make $30,000 to $40,000 a year. If you do a good job, maybe you're rewarded with a 2% bonus at the end of the year – 5% if you did a really good job. Now, if it was a bad year for retail, the owner has to absorb those losses and costs. But if the shop increased sales and revenue by, say, 50% in a given year – perhaps because of your own efforts – the owner can pay herself the full increase, which could easily run to several hundred thousand extra dollars.

Yes, there are risks. But there are also no limits on what an owner can earn. None. And, by the way, while that owner was on her business trip to Milan, she took a side trip to the magical Amalfi Coast of Italy and enjoyed the good life for a few weeks. The whole time spent sipping Brunellos and staring out at the sea, while money was rolling into her bank account courtesy of that highly capable manager she hired years ago. She may never come back.

When someone approached her about opening a second location – which they would pay to set up – taking advantage of the discounts she had negotiated out of her overseas suppliers, she agreed to the offer. Then, because of the increased size of her orders, she was able to get even better discounts from her suppliers. Of course, she kept a piece of the second store's profits in perpetuity. As long as both outlets do well, she is making great money even when she is not actually working. This is called Passive Income. And that's Financial Freedom. It is a truly beautiful thing: someone else puts in the effort and you reap the profits.

Some people listen to all this and say that while it sounds great to eliminate the limits on their earning potential, it all comes with a LOT of work. We've all heard stories of entrepreneurs working 80+ hour weeks to get their business up and running. And it's true. Great businesses don't come without a lot of work. So here's something else to consider: your motivation. Are you looking for a business – any business – that will make you rich, or are you trying to build something that you have a passion for? There is a huge difference. If you're just in it for the money, all that extra time and effort may start to wear you down, particularly if it takes several years to make a profit. But, imagine the scenario of building something you're passionate about. Let's say you absolutely love fashion. You spend your leisure time following the industry's top bloggers, reading all the magazines and watching the fashion shows. Now you start building a retail location with a strong online presence to bring your vision of fashion to customers who will appreciate your ideas. It will still take huge amounts of time, but it's no longer work in the traditional sense. Now you're having fun. And who cares if you have to invest twice as many hours a week as the average employee to establish your business? You're making ten times the salary of your manager, and having the time of your life doing it!

> **If you love what you do, you will never work a day in your life.**
>
> Confucius

## Consider This:

Instead of the typical employee's mindset of working 40 hours a week for 40 years, isn't it better to own the right kind of business, working 80+ hours a week for three to seven years, **and then never having to work again?**

So, why aren't we all entrepreneurs? It has a lot to do with our school system, which does a terrific job at preparing people for life as a worker bee. There's nothing wrong with worker bees; we need highly trained people to build roads, hospitals, cars and flat screen TVs. Ironically, North America was built by entrepreneurs. All the major advances in technology and lifestyle came about because someone had an idea about a better way of doing something, and then took the risk of developing that idea. Think of Thomas Edison, Henry Ford, Alexander Graham Bell, and more recently, Steve Jobs and Jeff Bezos. But schools, colleges and universities don't teach that approach, or that way of thinking. And, by the way, where are all the women on that list? What limiting messages have we been sending young girls for generations?

# Financial Freedom

Traditional education did, however, fill one need; Edison, Ford and Jobs all had a huge need for workers. But we are now living in a completely different economy and companies cannot hire someone and retain them for 40 years until retirement the way they used to. Five years or less is becoming a more common job lifespan. The world is rapidly changing, and companies are being disrupted by forces beyond their control. Kodak, for instance, was the iconic brand of film for cameras for most of the last century. They obviously weren't 'focused' on the future, or they would have invested more resources in developing digital cameras. That might have saved them, but they didn't do it, so their Japanese competitors seized the opportunity and basically put Kodak out of business – costing 78,000 people their jobs. Then, of course, the mobile phone started to replace the digital camera as the primary device for capturing memories and moments. How many people saw that coming?

## Facts of Life

As we move toward 2020 we need to be aware that:

- People have been conditioned to seek a guarantee in pay, but the reality is that the only guarantee is that your pay growth is severely limited and that you can be let go anytime at the whim of your boss.

- Society has done a great job promoting the myth that the goal is to WORK for a really good company. We say the goal should be to OWN a really good company.

- Adopting the entrepreneurial life is no longer just a choice some people make; it's now a matter of survival.

- The modern formula for success: applied financial literacy + the perfect business opportunity + the commitment to do the needed work = Financial Freedom.

The job "security" of the last century is long gone. Anyone clinging to that illusion will have a very rude awakening someday soon. Even those with a perceived stable job within a "stable" company could find themselves out on the street, replaced by someone who was thinking and acting more entrepreneurially, and thus representing a greater asset to the company.

So, what to do? Take comfort that in the final section of this book we have a list of 20 criteria that you can use to score the longevity and success potential of any business opportunity.

Providing consulting services for companies has been a big part of our practice, and has also offered us a great opportunity to learn about different approaches to business. We've personally interviewed hundreds of self-made millionaires and several billionaires. As a group they are very sharp, innovative thinkers, and we have witnessed how they confront emerging challenges and turn them into even more profits. When we started to look at these people as a group, studying what drove them and what made them think the way they did, we noticed they all personified certain traits. This realization was the inspiration for the ABCs philosophy. First and foremost, and without exception, we saw that this extremely diverse group shared a number of winning Attitudes, and that these Attitudes set them apart. From these successful people, we saw that you simply cannot be successful if you are weighed down by self-limiting Attitudes and Beliefs. Moreover, self-limiting Attitudes and Beliefs are fatal regardless of how hard you work, or how great your ideas are. Therefore, before we look at different business approaches and opportunities, and before we look at whether you should start your own business from scratch, buy into an existing business, join a direct marketing opportunity or purchase a franchise, we need to go back to the basics. Specifically, we need you to honestly ask yourself whether your day-to-day beliefs support success – or set you up for failure. All the training and development in the world will not guarantee you success unless you have the right Attitude.

**The greatest discovery of any generation is that a human can alter his life by altering his attitude.**

William James

# Financial Freedom

When you think of Financial Freedom, what image comes to mind? For us, because we come from the northern part of the country, thoughts invariably turn to palm trees and beaches after a few months of experiencing the awesome power of winter, and we become very receptive to work assignments or vacations in warm places. In our experience, rich and successful people see a lot more palm trees than snowplows. So, when we thought about images for the cover of this book, a tropical beach said Financial Freedom to us. You may be different. You may live in Florida or California where palm trees are common all year. What is a Financial Freedom image to you? Maybe it's a sleek car or a beautiful mansion. Whatever it is, use it as your display photo on your mobile, and your profile pic on your favorite social media sites. Print out a copy and paste it right into this book. Then hang up another copy somewhere you can easily see it. That's your visual inspiration to stay the course, to do the necessary work, and to move towards your dream of Financial Freedom.

In the space below, describe your image of Financial Freedom.

_____

_____

Now that you have an image in mind, what's your definition of Financial Freedom?

## My Definition of Financial Freedom:

_____

_____

Now that you have created your definition, and you have an image of it, you know your "why". Your "why" is what clarifies your focus, helps you overcome self-doubts, fears, negative messages and the adversities of life. It is a very powerful concept that will be covered in more detail later in this section.

## The ABC Guys' Definition of Financial Freedom:

> Having an abundance of choice to do what you want,
> when you want, where you want, and
> with whom you want.

Business owner Bob Graham offers his definition: "Having enough investments so you never have to work another day for the rest of your life". Have you got a great definition for Financial Freedom that you would like to share? Email it to us at **info@abcguys.com**

# Your Entrepreneurial Potential Self-Assessment

Do you currently share the winning attitudes typical of financially free entrepreneurs? Let's do the following assessment. This assessment includes 25 statements, and will only take about 5-10 minutes to complete. There are no right or wrong answers. Your honest opinion is what counts. Do not jump over this exercise, because you will miss out on a fundamental learning stage in your entrepreneurial journey and thereby jeopardize the achievement of your dreams.

Read the **Entrepreneurial Statements** in the table below and rate the degree to which you agree or disagree with each in the **Rating** column. Rate each statement as follows: 1= "disagree totally," 2="disagree somewhat," 3= "neither agree nor disagree," 4= "agree somewhat, and 5 = "agree totally." Avoid entering "3" whenever possible because this fence-straddling response will not allow you to benefit fully from the analysis. The **Develop** column on the far right is a place for you to jot down ideas as to how you might work on developing a more entrepreneurial Attitude regarding a specific statement.

# Financial Freedom

| Entrepreneurial Statements | Rating | Develop |
|---|---|---|
| I deserve to win in business and life. | | |
| I have a clear & concise mental picture of my goals. | | |
| I am my best asset & constantly seek ways to improve myself. | | |
| I keep my ego in check and I am coachable. | | |
| I make decisions confidently. | | |
| I don't work for money, money works for me. | | |
| I don't believe that you have to come from money to be financially free. | | |
| I enjoy helping others & I have a serving mindset. | | |
| I am prepared to put in the necessary work to achieve my goals. | | |
| I enjoy building relationships and positively influencing others. | | |
| I react well under pressure. | | |
| I maintain a healthy paranoia and avoid complacency. | | |
| Where others see problems, I see opportunities. | | |
| I am results driven & live with a sense of urgency. | | |
| I know that I create my own luck & future. | | |
| I enjoy taking calculated risks. | | |
| Failures are learning opportunities to me. | | |
| I believe that I can accomplish anything I put my mind to. | | |
| I am able to easily adapt to an ever-changing environment. | | |
| I am persistent and tenacious in achieving my goals. | | |
| I am a positive and optimistic person. | | |
| I like to compete and I am motivated by winning. | | |
| I know my key business numbers every day. | | |
| I am ready to seize opportunities 24/7 not just 9 to 5. | | |
| I like helping people around me win in business and in life. | | |

When you have competed the assessment, go back through each statement and note the rating you provided. Any rating of "4" or "5" is a positive response and indicates a Belief or Attitude that should be nurtured and further enhanced over time. Any rating of "3" is an opportunity to improve your entrepreneurial mindset. Ratings of 3 or less indicate a self-limiting belief that will greatly limit your potential if allowed to persist.

Clearly, the point of this exercise is learning how to turn a limiting belief into a supporting Attitude. You can do this by the following steps. First, you must face the facts. Turning inward and identifying self-limiting Attitudes takes effort, honesty, and courage. It's not an easy thing for most people to do. The upside is that you will be able to enjoy much more success in your future if you can break free of your Attitudinal handicaps.

Transcending your own self-limiting Attitudes begins with taking responsibility for them. What does taking responsibility mean? The essential element is revealed by the two parts of the word, "response" and "ability." If you can develop the ability to respond to a crippling belief by replacing it with something empowering, you have increased the likelihood of being able to take advantage of the hidden opportunities that come your way.

Once you have identified limiting Beliefs or Attitudes, don't get all tied up in knots about them. Let it go; forgive yourself. From the perspective of achieving Financial Freedom, past failures should be seen only as opportunities for learning and personal growth. Indeed, one of the best ways to live a productive life in general is to consciously choose to see the positive in everything, and to see it with an Attitude of gratitude. This will seem foreign, unnatural and uncomfortable for most people in the beginning. Our advice to such people: the more uncomfortable it feels, the more you need to start living this way.

At this point you are ready to start working on changing specific Attitudes. Select the lowest scoring Attitude from the 25 above and, without blaming anyone or anything, try to understand how that Attitude was formed. Was it based on feedback from a trusted person who has become financially free themselves? If not, it's time to reconsider that Attitude.

# Financial Freedom

> **Before accepting the message, validate the messenger.**
>
> ABC Guys

Our advice is to seek out positive role models and coaches whom you want to emulate. Make personal connections with them, read their books, or follow them on social media. Actively examine how they think and act regarding the specific Attitude you are working on. Before long their example will start rubbing off on you. The following tool is designed to help you change a limiting Attitude to an empowering one.

Insert your limiting Attitude below:

_____

_____

Previous Attitude regarding this mindset:

_____

_____

What has this Attitude cost you so far in your life?

_____

_____

What would your life look like without this limiting Belief?

_____

_____

# Financial Freedom

How is this change in Attitude going help you reach your goal of Financial Freedom?

_____

_____

What changes are you prepared and committed to make to reach your goal of Financial Freedom?

_____

_____

What is your new Attitude regarding this mindset:

_____

_____

> **If it doesn't challenge you, it doesn't change you.**
>
> Fred DeVito

## Mental Toughness

As we work with clients around the world, we are inundated with "How" questions. Typical how questions are: How can I increase my profits? How can I reduce employee turnover? How can I negotiate better deals? and so on. Although these are good questions, we feel that the more important questions entrepreneurs should be asking are "Why" questions, questions like *Why should I own my own company? or Why am I in this industry?*

"Why" questions typically require more holistic answers and compel us to examine our business relative to our dreams. A question like Why am I in business? should lead to a reexamination of personal goals and dreams. If your business doesn't directly provide a vehicle to fulfill your dreams, we would say that you are on the wrong track. For many people, their business and the freedom associated with it is the dream.

We often hear variations on the basic question of *How can I remain disciplined and do what I need to do to succeed in business?* The people who ask this question are stating that they find maintaining entrepreneurial discipline difficult, and that procrastination is all too easy in the face of a world of distractions. We respond to such people by saying that the very *opposite* is actually nearer the truth, that being disciplined is very easy and natural under the right circumstances.

How can we say this? Before answering this critical question, we must share our definition of discipline.

## DID YOU KNOW

Discipline is doing the **right thing**, at the **right time**, for the **right reason**. Procrastination, on the other hand, is the failure to do the right thing, at the right time, for the right reason.

We often share the following analogy during our workshops and public appearances to illustrate our ideas about discipline. We begin by asking our audience whether they can relate to a lack of sleep caused by taking care of a newborn baby. We ask them to think back on their experiences with their own children, siblings or relatives, and to recall how disruptive babies can be to the sleep patterns of an entire household, particularly when the child is sick, colicky or teething.

An upset baby means no one within earshot gets quality sleep. The primary caregivers do their best to comfort the baby, making sure the child is well fed, has a clean diaper, and generally doing everything possible to settle the little one down in their crib. And finally, when the child does drift back off to sleep, everybody in the household is sternly reminded that there will be grave consequences if anyone disturbs the baby. At this point everyone is silently praying that the all-merciful Creator will grant them just a few, sweet hours of sleep. But all too often the baby resumes crying the instant the caregiver's head hits the pillow.

At this point of excruciating fatigue, does the caregiver think, *well I'll just ignore the baby and hope it doesn't die?* Or does he or she call a friend or coach for guidance? No, they do what every rational, caring person would do: they get out of bed and do what they can to comfort their child.

The point here is that everyone responsible for an infant would do the right thing (get out of bed and comfort the baby), at the right time (right away because the child is not well) and for the right reason (love). You are naturally disciplined to do whatever you must to care for your child because you love them.

This principle also holds true for athletes who push their bodies to the limit as well as for entrepreneurs who seemingly sacrifice themselves for their business. Parents, athletes and business people tap into an inner strength to maintain the discipline necessary to act out the love they feel for their child, their sport, or their business. In short, we are suggesting that entrepreneurs fall in love with their business. Like the selfless parent of a crying baby, if you're truly in love with your business, procrastination will not become an issue because discipline becomes a natural daily occurrence.

For more help on improving your daily disciplines, check out Og Mandino's book *The World's Greatest Salesman*.

**Dreams are what get you started; daily disciplines get you to the goal.**

ABC Guys

# Financial Freedom

## Dream Accountability Tool

My dream is_____

In order to achieve my dream I have to commit to the following disciplines/activities this month.

| Disciplines | 01 | 02 | 03 | 04 | 05 | 06 | 07 | 08 | 09 | 10 | 11 | 12 | 13 | 14 | 15 | 16 | 17 | 18 | 19 | 20 | 21 | 22 | 23 | 24 | 25 | 26 | 27 | 28 | 29 | 30 | 31 |
|---|---|---|---|---|---|---|---|---|---|---|---|---|---|---|---|---|---|---|---|---|---|---|---|---|---|---|---|---|---|---|---|
|  |  |  |  |  |  |  |  |  |  |  |  |  |  |  |  |  |  |  |  |  |  |  |  |  |  |  |  |  |  |  |  |  |
|  |  |  |  |  |  |  |  |  |  |  |  |  |  |  |  |  |  |  |  |  |  |  |  |  |  |  |  |  |  |  |  |  |
|  |  |  |  |  |  |  |  |  |  |  |  |  |  |  |  |  |  |  |  |  |  |  |  |  |  |  |  |  |  |  |  |  |
|  |  |  |  |  |  |  |  |  |  |  |  |  |  |  |  |  |  |  |  |  |  |  |  |  |  |  |  |  |  |  |  |  |
|  |  |  |  |  |  |  |  |  |  |  |  |  |  |  |  |  |  |  |  |  |  |  |  |  |  |  |  |  |  |  |  |  |
|  |  |  |  |  |  |  |  |  |  |  |  |  |  |  |  |  |  |  |  |  |  |  |  |  |  |  |  |  |  |  |  |  |
|  |  |  |  |  |  |  |  |  |  |  |  |  |  |  |  |  |  |  |  |  |  |  |  |  |  |  |  |  |  |  |  |  |
|  |  |  |  |  |  |  |  |  |  |  |  |  |  |  |  |  |  |  |  |  |  |  |  |  |  |  |  |  |  |  |  |  |
|  |  |  |  |  |  |  |  |  |  |  |  |  |  |  |  |  |  |  |  |  |  |  |  |  |  |  |  |  |  |  |  |  |
|  |  |  |  |  |  |  |  |  |  |  |  |  |  |  |  |  |  |  |  |  |  |  |  |  |  |  |  |  |  |  |  |  |

## Instructions:

1. Write your 10 daily disciplines that will fast track you to achieving your dream in the space provided.

2. Each day, check the box after fully completing that discipline to track your progress.

3. The objective is to fill in all of the boxes during the month. You may elect to be "off" on certain days as long as it doesn't derail your process.

Are you ready to commit yourself to overcome the temptations of procrastination and to consistently fulfill your daily disciplines?

Yes _____     No _____

**If yes, sign here:** _____

**Supportive Person's signature:** _____

# Financial Freedom

## All He Wanted Was Freedom

In 1971, W. Mitchel moved to San Francisco to escape his small, mid-west hometown. He got his first job as cable car operator and saved his money for a dream motorbike, which represented freedom to him. One day, while out enjoying his new bike he drove too fast down a steep road; a truck cut him off and he lost his balance. Observers said it was like watching a horror movie: the bike fell over on top of him as he continued to skid downhill, the cap popped off the gas tank, and sparks ignited the gas.

He woke up in hospital a week later from a medically induced coma in unbelievable pain. Sixty-five percent of his body was covered with second and third degree burns, he lost most of his fingers, and was told that he would never be able to ride a bike again. The pain, disfigurement, and loss of freedom drove him into a deep depression in which he was constantly tormented by the question, why me lord? After several weeks of wallowing in "severe self-pity mode," he decided that he would not live the rest of his life in misery. After considerable soul searching, he reframed his mental outlook. From that point on, he lived his life in the light of a principle, which he expressed as, "It's not what happens to you, it's what you choose to do about it that matters."

Motivated by his need for freedom, he not only figured out how to adapt his bike so that he could ride it, but he also set the goal of one day purchasing and learning to fly a plane.

He had also always wanted to own a business and, as strange as it sounds, in 1972 he co-founded a small company that made efficient, airtight wood stoves and fireplaces. By 1974, Vermont Castings was becoming a very successful business. As it grew, he hired and coached a number of very talented people to run the day-to-day business. He figured out that his not having to work in the business on a daily basis provided him a source of passive income. This Financial Freedom provided him the means to seek other opportunities, to engage in causes he believed in, as well to purchase his dream airplane and obtain his single engine pilot license.

At that time, W. was living in Crested Butte, Colorado. The city's mayor, bolstered by a groundswell of public support, was then promoting an idea to boost jobs by developing a new mine. When W. researched the track record of the mining company and the detailed proposal they had presented to council, he found many errors in job predictions. Moreover,

# Financial Freedom

he was concerned that the proposed strip mine would destroy the mountain, harm the environment, and jeopardize the high value, tourism-based economy.

He decided to take matters into his own hands. With the single platform issue of defeating the mining proposal, he ran for and was elected to mayor in the next election. The focal point of his campaign was the promise of holding a referendum regarding the proposed mine. The referendum was held, the mining proposal was defeated, and W. was credited with saving the mountain.

Several months after becoming mayor, on his first flight in his new airplane, he and two passengers were exploring the mountain and surrounding area for additional economic opportunities. Tragically, the plane was caught in a sudden crosswind and crashed into the side of the mountain. Although his two passengers walked away, W. was not so lucky. Waking up days later in traction, with several broken bones and permanent spinal cord damage, W. received the devastating news that he would never walk again. To make matters even more intolerable, his wife left him, saying that she "could never be tied down to a crippled, burnt French fry! "With his freedom gone, his wife abandoning him, and the ever-present pain, he seriously considered suicide. But once again, he dug down deep inside and decided, "the pity-party is over, it's not what happened to me, it's what I choose to do about it!"

After deciding not to give up and be a victim, he sold his shares in his business for $65 million, and bought several investment properties that provided a massive passive income. After some time he met and married a woman who truly loved him, and went on to write several inspirational best-selling books. He now speaks all over the world, sharing his powerful message, "that freedom is not riding a bike, or flying a plane; it is a state of mind. In life, it's not what happens to you, it's what you choose to do about it that matters!"

Life is filled with adversity, and starting a business is no different. Some people might ridicule you for going into business, challenging your ability to succeed. Others might join you, but then either fail to perform or even betray you. Clients might back out just before you finalize an agreement, or immediately switch to a competitor, while spreading lies about you and your business over the social media. Expect adversity to happen because it will. The key is not what happens, but how you deal with it.

> **"** Strength doesn't come from what you
> can do, it comes from overcoming things
> you thought you could not do.
>
> Rickki Rogers **"**

## Get Comfortable With Selling

At this point you might think that selling is not an issue; *I'll get someone else to do it for me*. This is highly flawed thinking. It's fine for businesses to have dedicated sales people, but if the business owner is uncomfortable or unskilled at selling and promoting the company and its products, the business is starting off with a huge handicap: a poor Attitude toward selling.

The fact is that there is no **business** until a sale is made. Without sales you don't have a business; you have, at best, a hobby or a charity. If you are not prepared to embrace selling, you simply won't succeed in business!

Everyone is good at selling when they're given the right motivation. For example, think back to when you wanted to get that other person you really liked to date you, or, think about the child who wants a cookie before dinner, or when you needed to unload an aging car to stop the financial hemorrhage.

Entrepreneurs are constantly selling and persuading. They sell to buyers, they sell their vision to their team, and they sell their ideas to investors. Effective entrepreneurs are constantly selling their business partners, suppliers, the media and their local community on just about everything they do. Even when you have a sales team doing the majority of customer sales, the entrepreneur needs to be an excellent salesperson if he or she is to build a long-term, profitable organization.

But if you think selling is something you can't do, don't give up and abandon your dream of owning a business and achieving Financial Freedom because selling can be a learned skill. Let's take a closer look at selling.

The reality is that sales and selling has gotten a bad reputation. Most people harbor stereotypes of manipulative, slick, pushy and downright dishonest salespeople. Sales techniques are often taught in training programs as something that you **do to someone** as opposed to something that you **do with and for someone**. We espouse the latter version and here's why.

We should start by sharing our own, expanded definition of selling: **"Selling is the process of influencing or persuading someone to your way of thinking"**. Selling is an ethically neutral act, neither good nor bad; it is the intentions and actions of the seller that make all of the difference. Just as in all other areas of business, there are honest and dishonest salespeople. Is the seller trying to manipulate the customer, or is he or she promoting a true win-win situation?

Assuming the seller's intentions are good, is this enough? We believe that there are at least two other critical elements. One is that the customer has a true need for the product or service, and the other is that the product or service is competitively priced. With these elements in place, you have the preconditions for a sale. What is required next is for the seller to be knowledgeable and passionate about the product.

Some commonly used words are loaded with negative connotations and could be taken out of context during a sales encounter.

| Word: | Consider Replacing With: |
| --- | --- |
| Tell | Explain; advise; share |
| You need to... | I'd like to suggest; would you reconsider? |
| Spend | Invest |
| Cost | Investment |
| Sales pitch | Presentation |
| Buy; purchase | Obtain; invest; own |
| Deal | Opportunity; transaction |
| Objections | Areas of concern |
| Problem | Challenge/ Opportunity |

If you have not invested the time or money to develop your sales skills and are looking for a primer, we would recommend you pick up the book *How to Master the Art of Selling* by Tom Hopkins. From there you can go on to seek out more advanced books and courses on the subject.

> **If you want something you have never had, you have to do something you have never done.**
>
> Unknown

## Overcoming Fear/Doubt

Whenever doubt or fear starts to creep into your mind regarding approaching people about your business, ask yourself the following four critical questions:

1.  Do you have a product, service or solution that can truly benefit people?

2.  Does your prospective customer have a real need for your product or service?

3.  Is your product or service competitively priced?

4.  Are you an honest person who cares about the well being of others?

If you can answer yes to all four questions, then you really need to get over your fears and doubts, and to talk to everyone you meet about how your product or service can improve their lives.

## Overcoming Adversity

Imagine being told that you will never walk again! That was what doctors told London-born Kieran Behan after they removed a cancerous tumor from his thigh at the age of 10. The operation went badly; so badly in fact, that he woke up screaming in pain from massive nerve damage. Up to then, he had been crazy about gymnastics and was determined to become an Olympic champion. But how could he do that when he was confined to a wheelchair?

But Kieran was unwilling to abandon his dream, so he started on the long road to recovery. He was confined to a wheelchair for 15 months, but thereafter he went right back to the gym. Unfortunately, after a few months he slipped from the high bar and sustained a terrible head injury. He was so badly injured that he suffered blackouts every time he blinked. He missed a whole year at school while recuperating, and then the gym began to beckon to him again. This time, however, he had to overcome neurological challenges as well as the damage to his leg. He had to retrain his brain to regain co-ordination. He returned to school using a cane, and was cruelly taunted by his classmates.

It took him three years to get back to where he had been before the accident. But then he suffered several more fractures. Another blow came when his knee snapped just after he had been selected for the European Championships. Behan recalls that was when he nearly gave up.

But he did not give up, and eventually succeeded in becoming the Challenge World Cup floor champion in 2011. Perhaps his greatest moments of glory were when he qualified for the London 2012 and the Rio 2016 Olympic Games.

During his routine at Rio, his left knee dislocated on his first tumble. He could have stopped right there, safe in the knowledge that nobody would even think twice about his decision, but he did not. He says of that moment, "It's one of those things. As soon as my feet touched the ground on that first tumble and the knee went, I just knew that it was about survival and just getting through the rest of the routine. I nearly stopped after the first move but, I just thought, go for it!" Kieran Behan's mental toughness embodies the Olympic spirit! And clearly, just a fraction of this toughness would go a very long way to helping anyone seeking Financial Freedom.

When a new business owner ask us for advice on how to deal with a "huge" setback, such as a disappointing teammate, or a sale that didn't go through in spite of a tremendous amount of preparation, we share a story like Kiernan's. Then we ask them to reread the beginning of this chapter. If you let the decisions of others derail your dreams, you haven't properly connected with your Why.

## Overcoming Adversity

When facing adversity don't wallow in negative thinking or host a pity party. Instead choose to **STEP** towards your goals right away.

**S**mile – Even if at first you don't feel like it. You will feel better and others will respond positively to you.

**T**alk positively – To yourself and everyone else and make sure that the negative thinking doesn't take root.

**E**nergize yourself – Get mentality and physically active by going outside, exercise, network with positive people or read a personal development book.

**P**roduce more results– Double your efforts towards your goal.

Speaking of potentially derailing your dreams, if you have a life partner, it is not necessary that they be in business with you, however it is critical that they are positive and supportive. Such a partner or spouse can really help you through the tough times of launching and running your new business. Unfortunately, the opposite is equally true. If your life partner does not fully support you then they will be constantly undermining your success by chipping away at your confidence. If this is the case then you really need to talk the issue through and see if you can achieve some kind of positive agreement.

# Financial Freedom

## Are You Coachable?

One of the most important predictors of the success of a new business is whether the owner is coachable. If you think you have all the answers, you're wrong – no matter how experienced, educated or street-smart you may be. The most successful people know how to listen to what others have to contribute. A smart leader likes to have his or her ideas challenged, and is open to suggestions on growing the business. Such a leader believes in life-long learning, consuming books and online videos by people who have faced and overcome similar challenges in the business world. These are the kind of people we can learn from.

Coaches are a critical component of any successful business. Identify someone from your chosen industry with a proven track record of success and approach them about becoming your coach. Obviously, you must be respectful of their time, and you must listen carefully to their advice. Also, be sure to tell them exactly what actions you took and how it helped you. You may be surprised at the high caliber of coach you can get, merely by asking.

## Negative People

Successful business people also know how to tune out negativity. Lots of people stuck in the employee mindset will be jealous or threatened by the new direction you've chosen. Members of your own family – perhaps even your own spouse or partner–may tell you in no uncertain terms that they think you're crazy. They may have friends who've failed at every business venture they tried, or they may consider themselves experts on the subject because of "something they read on the Internet." By all means hear them out and consider their comments, especially if they have an evidence-based argument. But ALWAYS be mindful of the source of the information. If you've done your research, asked the tough business questions, and have not found anyone knowledgeable who can point to any fatal flaws, then tune out the naysayers; you've found a real opportunity! As we've always said, if you find yourself surrounded by negative people, don't just walk away from them, **run away** from them!

# DID YOU KNOW

Although the Internet can be a fantastic source of information you can't afford to accept every comment as accurate. A recent search of some very popular topics yielded an astonishing amount of negative comments. The real danger would be to simply write off someone or something just because of some unfavorable online comments. Conduct some more in-depth research to obtain the truth.

| Topic: | # Negative Comments |
| --- | --- |
| Starbucks | 528,000 |
| Mother Teresa | 40,100,000 |
| Santa Claus | 91,900,000 |
| Wal-Mart | 778,000 |
| Easter Bunny | 119,000 |
| Puppies | 550,000 |
| Health Food | 9,370,000 |

A Cherokee elder is teaching his grandson about life. "A fight is going on inside me," he says to the boy. "It is a terrible fight, and it is between two wolves. One is evil, filled with anger, envy, sorrow, regret, greed, arrogance, self-pity, guilt, resentment, inferiority, lies, false pride, superiority, and ego. The other is good – he is filled with joy, peace, love, hope, serenity, humility, kindness, benevolence, empathy, generosity, truth, compassion, and faith. The same fight is going on inside you – and inside every other person, too."

# Financial Freedom

The grandson thinks about his grandfather's words for a moment. Then he asks, "Which wolf will win?"

The old man smiles gently and looks his grandson in the eye. "The one you feed," he replies.

"You must associate yourself with positive winners," says Financially Free business owner, Michael Sharpe. Over three decades, Michael has modeled this Attitude, illustrating how to remove negative and cynical people from your life. "When negativity takes root in your organization, it's like a cancer. It spreads and there is no cure except radical surgery."

Our thoughts can be our own worst enemy. That is, they can be our nemesis if we let them. Think about how you may be "feeding and watering" your negative thoughts by allowing them to rule your mind. Consider catching the next negative thought that pops up and then ask yourself: *What is this line of thinking doing for me?* You will almost certainly discover that its only definite impact is to dis empower you; to pull the plug on your engine of action. Now consider the opposite: what does it feel like when you think about something that is unquestionably good, like arranging for those ballet lessons your sweet little grand-daughter has been pining for? Not only does this thought trigger a rush of tender emotion, it positively fires you up! You instantly feel a need to make those dancing lessons continue to happen – and you check your schedule to see if you can be chauffeur as well as financier.

They may feel artificial at first, but directing your mind to positive areas feeds real actions that only need the watering of attention to bloom. Fear is the enemy of success, and if you're ruled by fear, you'll never take the right risks and never achieve Financial Freedom. We can create greater peace, confidence and a more positive outlook by learning how to manage our thoughts. This battle can be won because we have the power of choice! **Which wolf are you feeding?**

## Be AWARE

Whenever you feel the negative impact of doubt, consider using the following tool to help regain self-control. The key point is to be *aware* of how doubt affects you, and to move beyond it towards your dreams. A powerful way to regain freedom from negativity and its gloomy consequences is the acronym AWARE:

**A**ccept that doubt and fear is natural; it happens to us all.

**W**atch out for doubt and fear. Don't let them operate unchallenged.

**A**ct quickly and choose the right Attitudes and Behaviors to move forward.

**R**e-connect and surround yourself with positive, like-minded people.

**E**nergize yourself by focusing on your dreams.

## Emotional Maturity

As the "Be AWARE" visual above reminds us, we need to be aware of our present situation, and choose the appropriate response. We all know people who have matured chronologically, but have never matured emotionally. These people's emotions are erratic, up one day (or minute) and down the next, and their lives seem to bounce from one drama to another. The dictionary defines maturity "as the ability to respond to the environment in an appropriate manner." Thus Emotional Maturity refers to the ability to consistently respond emotionally in an appropriate manner.

Business owner Bill Whittle, who is also a coach to thousands of people, often speaks about the importance of Emotional Maturity for leaders. He uses the following illustration as an example, "Imagine having two buckets: one filled with gasoline and the other water. Life provides moments of truth when you have a choice: do you use the gas and accelerate the flames or do you extinguish the flames with the water? The situation dictates the appropriate response. We all know people, some very intimately, who should have chosen the water to pour on the flames of doubt, fear, anger, hatred, and tension, when instead they used the bucket of gas and the flames went ablaze! We also know people who should have chosen the bucket of gas to ignite the flame of excitement, fun, belief, love, loyalty, or passion, but instead extinguished the flame with the water."

By managing our emotions appropriately we impact the people we are dealing with and ourselves. The more we mature emotionally, the more likely we will move consistently toward our goals and Financial Freedom.

# DID YOU KNOW

The Chinese have an interesting symbol for the word "change". It is comprised of two parts: danger and opportunity. Change is inevitable; how we choose to see it and react to it makes all the difference. This is a powerful Attitude.

## Goal Setting

If the first part of achieving Financial Freedom is developing a winning Attitude and eliminating self-limiting Beliefs, then the second component is knowing where to focus your efforts – in other words, defining your Goals. If your goal is to be "successful" or "rich," that's nice, but it's too vague. You can end up going down several different paths and never getting to your goal. Why? Because **you can't hit a target you can't see**. The benefit of goal setting is that it converts wishful thinking into reality. Goal setting gives you direct influence over your future by creating a focus and a direction for your efforts. In turn, this focus increases your odds of actually achieving your goal as well as spotting other opportunities along the way. If, for example, your goal is to find a high-traffic retail space in an area receptive to your products or services, you are more likely to mention that to other people, one of whom may know of a perfect space that's just become available.

You can break your dream down into sub-goals, each dependent on the achievement of its predecessor. If, for example, you want to open a retail shop, you might want to begin with researching and establishing relationships with a group of distributors. Give yourself a deadline and get going. The next step might be finding the right location. Again, set a deadline and get going. With a store and suppliers in line, you now need to set a deadline for coming up with money for rent and merchandise. This is an example of the sequence and scheduling of goals that every new entrepreneur needs to go through.

In setting goals, we recommend the **S.M.A.R.T.** method of goal setting. We like this method because it's really easy to understand and use. S.M.A.R.T. is an acronym for the characteristics every good goal should have. Specifically, good goals should be Specific, Measurable, Attainable, Realistic, and Time-defined. So, let's say you want to open that retail shop, or you want to start a consulting business. A Specific goal would be to establish relations with a few distributors over the next three weeks; or to have three new consulting clients signed up within the next three months. Now you have a Specific Goal and a Timeline in which to accomplish it. The next question is whether that goal is Attainable? Do you have the background or credentials required in order for someone to take you seriously? Do you need to take some courses first, or establish a line of credit? Is the goal Realistic? Can you do it in three weeks/months, or is twice that time more Realistic? Finally, the outcome must be clearly measurable, either quantitatively or qualitatively, if you are to know the true measure of your success.

We want you to be successful, so we urge you to use this model to focus and define your goals. Using the **S.M.A.R.T.** model, you are not only more likely to achieve your goal; you will know where you went wrong if you are not successful on your first try.

# Financial Freedom

> Obstacles are those frightening things
> you see the moment you take your
> eyes off the goal.
>
> Henry Ford

## Sample S.M.A.R.T. Goal Action Plan
### Goal: Set up a three-month emergency fund. (This is something everyone should have).

| | |
|---|---|
| Day One: | Discuss goal with partner or spouse |
| Day Two: | Speak to boss regarding automatic payroll deductions. |
| Day Three: | Gather information on available investment funds. |
| Day Four: | You and your spouse meet with a financial adviser and set up an investment account. |
| Day Five: | Take lunch to work. |
| | After dinner conduct credit card cutting ceremony. |
| Day Six: | Review past week's accomplishments and celebrate. |
| Day Seven: | Day off – rest. |
| Week Two: | Get ride to work, car pool, or use public transportation for at least one day to save on gas and parking. |
| Week Three: | Find other cost cutting measures. |
| Week Four: | Review past month's efforts, revise next month's plan if necessary. Celebrate successes to date. |

The last part of Goal Setting is Accountability. There's no point in setting goals if you're not going to keep them and, with all the distractions that surrounded us, it's easy to be thrown off course. Take a few minutes and customize the following template making space to list all your necessary actions, then print it off and sign it. If possible, have your spouse, partner, business associate or friend co-sign it and allow them to keep a copy and hold you accountable. Then, set up some reminders – daily, weekly – on your smart phone so that you regularly review your progress. If one of your steps takes longer than estimated that's OK. You'll have to rework your plan and timelines, then print it off and discuss again with your co-signee.

# Financial Freedom

| My Accountability Timeline | |
|---|---|
| My Dream: | |

| Actions: | Completed |
|---|---|
| This week:<br>1<br>2<br>3 | ☐ Yes!<br>☐Yes!<br>☐Yes! |
| Week two:<br>1<br>2<br>3 | ☐Yes!<br>☐Yes!<br>☐Yes! |
| One month from now I will have accomplished:<br>1<br>2<br>3 | ☐Yes!<br>☐Yes!<br>☐Yes! |
| Six months from now I will have accomplished:<br>1<br>2<br>3 | ☐Yes!<br>☐Yes!<br>☐Yes! |
| One Year from now I will have accomplished:<br>1<br>2<br>3 | ☐Yes!<br>☐Yes!<br>☐Yes! |
| Five Years from now I will have accomplished:<br>1<br>2<br>3 | ☐Yes!<br>☐Yes!<br>☐Yes! |
| By signing below I agree to be held accountable for accomplishing everything above and encourage my co-signee to hold me to this agreement.<br>Signature_____Co-Signed by _____ | |

At this point we hope you've replaced any fears you might have had about starting your own business, dropped any self-limiting Beliefs, and set some realistic entrepreneurial goals. If you feel you are at this point, then you're ready to start examining some of the mechanics of putting your plan into action and achieving Financial Freedom.

# Financial Freedom

## Section Two: Behaviors That Create Financial Freedom

In this section we want to look at some of the basics of setting up a new business. Specifically, we'll consider raising and managing money and developing winning relationships with clients and teammates. We will address these issues under the heading of The 7 R's – **Raising capital**, building **Relationships**, getting **Referrals**, **Recruiting** great people, **Retaining** productive teammates, providing **Recognition**, and building future leaders through **Replication**.

## Raising Capital to Start Your Business

You might have heard of the old saying that it takes money to make money. There is some truth to this statement. Don't, however, reject a business opportunity simply because it comes with a huge price tag attached to it. We will cover this more in the next section. All businesses do require some start-up capital, and this requirement can be one of the greatest challenges for would be entrepreneurs. Some enterprises can be launched with modest funds while others may require millions in upfront investments.

To better understand the different sources of raising capital for business startups, let's first break them down by type, detailing the pros and cons of each. Financing generally comes in four forms: Personal Investment, Debt, Equity, Crowd Funding or Grants.

## Keeping Your Own House in Order

We would be doing you a huge disservice by not taking a minute to discuss the management of your personal finances before discussing raising capital for a new business. The first step in analyzing your personal finances is to assess your spending and saving habits in terms of the following chart. To rate yourself, enter a number that most accurately describes you right now, where the numbers 1 through 5 represent, respectively, "never," "rarely," "as often yes as no," "sometimes," and "always." Then score yourself, using the key at the bottom of the page.

# Financial Freedom

| Snapshot of my personal Financial Freedom. | |
|---|---|
| **Financial Statement** | **Rating (1 – 5)** |
| This month's bills arrive before I can pay off last month's bills. | |
| I always seem to have some unopened bills or notices. | |
| I receive at least three cut-off or past due notices per year. | |
| I never have enough emergency money saved to cover 3 months of lost income. | |
| My family would experience a huge financial crisis if I died tomorrow. | |
| My spouse/partner and I never outline our financial plans/ goals in writing. | |
| My spouse/partner has no idea how much it costs us to live on a monthly basis. | |
| I or my spouse/partner keeps a negative running balance in my/our checkbook. | |
| I prefer purchasing products that I can buy with a minimal down payment. | |
| I often seem to be short a few dollars and borrow money from friends/relatives. | |
| My credit card balances are usually near the maximum credit line. | |
| I bounce more than three checks per year. | |
| I often worry or get depressed about my financial situation. | |
| I experience some form of health problems or lack of sleep due to financial stress. | |
| I often argue with my spouse/partner about money matters. | |
| More than 20% of my net monthly income goes toward installment payments. | |
| I find myself saying *If I only made 10% more money all problems would disappear*. | |
| I often find myself making excuses or blaming others for my financial situation. | |
| I feel "out of control" as it relates to money matters. | |
| I feel that "I don't know what the first step is" in resolving my money concerns. | |

# Financial Freedom

Your score is simply the sum of the ratings. Interpret your score as follows:

**Score of 20 – 30.** Your Financial Fitness Indicator (or "score") is quite positive. You are on the right track, and your primary objective should be to fine-tune your strategies and fast-track your wealth building.

**Score of 31 – 45.** Your score is slightly better than average. Although you are doing more things right than wrong, there certainly are areas that warrant improvement. Your main objective should be review your weaker areas and resolve to improve them.

**Score over 45.** Your score is poor. But don't despair, you are not alone, and the next section will be very helpful to you. If you need more help, many other resources are available (our contributions to Financial Literacy are listed below). Seek them out.

Yes, the above exercise can be sobering, but it is really important that you do it, especially if you're thinking about opening your own business. You see, if you haven't learned the skills to balance your personal checkbook, the chances of succeeding in your own business are slim at best! You might be able to secure some loans or investments, only to realize that you have wasted other people's money as well. The good news is that your shaky financial situation can be corrected, and it won't even be that painful to do so. Moreover, good financial habits in the home usually extend to your business activities. It just requires a little reorganization and discipline.

For most people, the answer to getting out of debt or saving up for something is simple: "I need a raise." But actually, a raise does not always solve the problem. There are three reasons for this. First, you may not get it when you ask for it. Second, a significant portion of the raise will be eaten up by taxes. Third and finally, the natural inclination when getting a raise is to go out and spend it on a celebration, or to purchase something you can't really afford but have been putting off buying for ages. The bottom line: you may actually be worse off financially than you were before the raise.

We've written extensively about achieving Financial Freedom in our other books, including *"The ABCs of Making Money," "The ABCs of Making Money for Teens,"* and *"Getting Rich, How to Avoid Being Ripped-Off by the Insurance Industry."* So if you need more help, please check them out for dozens of ideas and really simple exercises to get your finances in order. For the purposes of this book, however, we're just going to summarize the basics.

## Living Within Your Means

The biggest challenge for most people is due to the fact that they simply don't know where their money goes. So clearly, the first step is to start tracking your spending. Other books we've written contain the world's simplest budgeting tools. Now we're going to break it down even further. (By the way, doing this exercise with your spouse or partner will make it that much more effective.)

Gather your monthly expenses together and write them down. We're going to divide them into three categories: Essentials; Non-Essentials, and Daily Living.

**Essentials.** The Essentials category covers items that are not really negotiable for most of us, such as rent or mortgage payments, car payments and driving expenses, taxes, life insurance (***never, ever buy anything other than term life insurance***), medical expenses, credit card debt, child care, tuition, and so on. If you can start to car-pool, or drop the kids off at a relative's place to save money, that's great. But the easier savings will come out of the next category.

**Non-essentials.** The list of items on the Non-Essentials comprises important, desirable items, but items that nevertheless might be reduced or eliminated in the service of achieving a greater goal. These include: Your cable/satellite package (do you really need all those channels?); mobile phones (can you get a better rate from a competitor, or reduce some of the add-ons?); magazine subscriptions; gym memberships; clothing; cigarettes; eating out, and so on.

Cutting back or eliminating some of these items may hurt a little; but some you will barely notice. But when you take those savings per month and multiply them by 12, you may be surprised at the potential yearly savings.

The third category is your **Daily Spending**. This one simply requires you to tally up what you spend every day for a week or two. Coffee (drink at home or the office for huge savings); lunch (Brown bag it, it's healthier too); newspapers; magazines; drinks after work, and so on. You may be surprised when you look back that a week's spending amounts to as much as it does. And we are certain that you will be surprised at how painlessly most of them can be reduced or even eliminated.

Upon completing this exercise, most are surprised to discover that they are able to save at least $100 a month (that's $1,200 a year and it's tax free), and to do so painlessly. The critical issue then becomes: what do you do next? The essential first step is to get aggressive with the payments on debts with the highest interest rates. That usually means your credit cards, which carry extortionist interest rates, making it hard to eliminate them completely. ("Pay Day" loans? Don't even think about it!) Once you've eliminated the most usurious debts, pay down any other debts – such as lines of credit. Mortgages can occasionally be renegotiated down to a cheaper rate, which is great, but if you're already paying in the range of 2.5% to even 5% for a mortgage, then your mortgage is not one of your biggest challenges. By all means accelerate your mortgage payments and start paying bi-weekly instead of monthly, and you'll save yourself years of costly payments.

When your debts are eliminated or at least under control, and once you have saved up a 3-month emergency fund, then it is time to start a "war chest" to finance part or all of your new enterprise. Remember, it's not how much you make; it's what you do with it that counts.

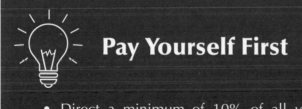

## Pay Yourself First

- Direct a minimum of 10% of all your earnings to investments (IRA & RSP's).

- Get out of debt ASAP.

- Establish a 3 – 6 month emergency fund.

## Personal Investment

Personal investment entails the use of the owner's own money to finance their business. The benefit of this approach is that there is no debt or sharing of equity. You take the risks, but you reap all of the rewards. Bootstrapping – investing as you go – is a great method to fund a small business. It starts with a modest investment from personal funds and, as the business proves itself by generating profits, the majority of the profits are reinvested into the business to finance the next stage of growth.

Obviously, the downside of personal investment is that most people simply don't have enough money, saved or invested, that can be allocated to starting a business. In this regard, people should not consider themselves capable of self-financing if doing so would require raiding their emergency fund, the education fund for their children, or their personal retirement account.

## Debt

Financing through debt means you borrow the money from someone and agree to pay it back at a certain date, or on an agreed schedule, along with some interest. The benefit is that you get the money upfront without using all or part of your personal funds. The downside is that lenders make their profit from the interest. So, over time you will have to pay back the principle amount and in many cases several times that in interest charges. The riskier your business is (which is to say, the higher the lender's assessment of the likelihood you won't pay back the loan), the higher the interest rate you will have to pay. One of the most dangerous traps to avoid is using credit cards to fund a business. Because credit card interest rates can be as high as 29.5%, many owners struggle just to make the interest payment while never retiring the debt. Worse still are "Pay Day" loan companies, most of which will charge you in the range of 600% for a short-term loan.

## Equity

An equity investment is when someone gives you money in exchange for partial ownership of your business. The more developed your business is, the more someone will have to pay you for that piece of ownership.

The benefit is that you obtain funding without using your personal funds or by generating debt. The downside is that you are diluting your equity – that is to say your ownership of the business. Let's say someone raised $10,000 by selling a 10% equity in their business. Imagine two years later when their business is worth $500,000. That 10% equity stake they sold two years earlier is now worth $50,000. Basically it cost you $50,000 to get $10,000 of funding. And if the value of the business continues to go up, so does the cost of the lost equity.

# DID YOU KNOW

The 12 questions most Venture Capitalists ask entrepreneurs seeking funding are as follows:

1. Why did you start this business?
2. What have you personally invested in the company?
3. Where do you see your company in three to five years?
4. What difficulties do you anticipate?
5. Who are your clients, how do you reach them, and how much does reaching them cost?
6. Who is your competition, and how will you compete with them?
7. How will you handle a bigger business if it enters your market?
8. What are my potential risks if I give you the money you want?
9. How much can my investment make?
10. When can I expect my money back, and how will you repay it?
11. What do you plan to do with the money you are requesting?
12. Will you require additional investments?

Some of these questions may sound onerous, but put yourself in their shoes: would you risk your money on a stranger? The key in answering these questions is to be fully prepared with intelligent, factual answers that demonstrate that you know your stuff and are a low investment risk. These people are interested in facts, not your dreams for a possible future.

## Crowd-Funding

Crowd-funding is the process of raising capital for a business or a business idea by using the Internet and various social media platforms to reach out to a large group of people. Crowd-funding can save time and money: Instead of doing endless rounds at banks and the offices of private investors, you can organize your Crowd-funding strategy very quickly. Often campaigns offer supporters products or services, so no debt or devaluation of equity occurs. An additional advantage is you can create a customer base and build awareness for your products or services at the same time as you raise startup money.

The downside to Crowd-funding is that it doesn't deliver for business-to-business offers because it focuses exclusively on consumers. Crowd-funding does not work for complex businesses ideas because of the limitation of the platform to share many details. Crowd-funding sites typically focus on projects requiring $100,000 or less in startup funds. If your idea requires more funding, you might need to consider looking at other, more traditional sources for raising capital. Most Crowd-funding platforms only release the funds once your campaign achieves 100% or more of its funding goal. This "all or nothing" approach can leave you stuck in limbo if your campaign fails to achieve its funding target. But it also makes your project inflexible: once you receive the funding, you cannot make drastic changes to your offering. Similarly, any delays in timelines could damage your reputation and hurt your brand. You also must bear in mind that the Crowd-funding platform will normally keep between 4 to 12% of all the funds raised as their commission. **Many industries are subject to specific regulations. Make sure before considering launching any crowd funding campaign that it is fully compliant.**

## Apply for Government Grants

If you work in biotech or other research-based industries, you might be able to get government support in the form of a grant. Cities with state college and university campuses also may have research centers and resources available to small business owners, especially those leading startups. Applying for a grant takes a tremendous amount of time and requires a well-prepared presentation of your business and submitting to a formal application process.

If your company's mission is closely tied to agencies such as the Department of Agriculture or the Department of Energy, the U.S. Small Business

Administration (SBA) or, in Canada, the Business Development Bank, can be another valuable resource. By contrast, a startup looking to fund a new retail store or launch a consumer smart phone app would probably find it more difficult to secure government dollars. But all three businesses also could turn to private-sector grants, if appropriate, from philanthropic organizations such as the Bill and Melinda Gates Foundation. It is the author's opinion that businesses need to stand on their own merits and that public funds should not be abused.

## Developing Lifelong Win/Win Relationships

> **Nobody cares how much you know until they know how you much care.**
>
> Cavett Roberts

Whatever type of business you decide to pursue, another key to success is your ability to build great relationships and rapport with suppliers, clients and teammates. On both sides of the equation, people like doing business with people they like. Thus, if you have a great relationship with a supplier, the supplier will be more likely to be accommodating when you need a few extra days on a payment so long as you don't make it a habit. We all know that customers will go out of their way to do business with a merchant they like. An organic butcher we know gives a good discount to all his regular customers, a"neighborhood discount,"as he calls it. A discount won't make up for a bad product, but this man consistently has a top-notch product, and gives repeat customers a few dollars off as well. He knows how to make his customers feel special and valued, and this is one reason they don't take their business elsewhere.

Building a rapport with your buyer very early in the sales process is also key. This can be accomplished by focusing on the buyer's needs versus the seller's. The seller has to ask many questions to encourage buyers to share their real needs, challenges and goals. One rapport-building technique that helps bond the two parties together is called matching and mirroring. In this technique, the seller takes the communication style lead from the buyer by observing the buyer's style of verbal and nonverbal communication. For instance, if a seller notices that the buyer is sitting erect and speaking in a low, slow voice, he would be well advised to "mirror" the buyer's body language and tone of voice, and to behave like the buyer in other obvious ways. The point is not to merely mimic the buyer, and certainly not to make fun of him, but to respect his communication style and to attempt to increase his comfort level by communicating in the same style. This approach, when used skillfully and with the right intention, places the buyer at ease and starts to build a sense of trust between both parties. With the emergence of trust and open dialogue, the seller will be able to learn the buyer's primary motivations in making a decision to buy.

Buying motivators can be expressed in many ways, but the two primary factors that influence every adult buying decision are: the avoidance of pain and/or the attainment of pleasure. If the seller can demonstrate how his or her product or service can help the buyer avoid some pain or attain some pleasure, the likelihood of building the relationship and making a sale will be very high. "Pain issues"include potential losses, missed opportunities, stress, and high costs; "pleasure issues " for buyers include increased profits or revenues, a sense of freedom, personal enjoyment, and an increased sense of personal worth. It is vital that the seller learn which primary buying motives are driving a buyer's purchasing decisions.

Here's an easy way to build instant rapport. We call it the LOVE technique and it functions by reminding you to ask questions about the things that people care about:

**L** – ask about their Loved ones.

**O** – ask about their Occupation.

**V** – ask about their recent Vacations, hobbies, and other interests.

**E** – ask about their Economic situation – taxes; feelings regarding new businesses..

Remember, to put some "LOVE" into your discussion because you're not (or should not) be trying to manipulate people. You should be trying to get them to open up so that you can both decide whether you want to do business with each other, and to try to determine whether you might be compatible in business over the long term.

In our opinion, the healthiest and most effective way to look at sales is the Relationship Selling Method as taught by Bill Gibson of KBI Training. The following chart illustrates the Five Phases of Relationship Selling, as adapted from Gibson's pioneering work in the field.

# 5 Relationship Development Stages – Financial Services Example

| | Attraction Stage "Watching" | Exploration Stage "Testing" | Development Stage "Bonding" | Committing Stage "Trusting" | Unconditional Commitment Stage |
|---|---|---|---|---|---|
| Friendship | A stranger | An Acquaintance | An Associate | A Friend | A Best Friend/ Partner |
| Intimate | Flirtation | Occasional Dates | Steady dating | Engagement | Marriage/ Partner |
| Business | Potential supplier | Short term supplier | Developing Supplier | Supplier of choice | Partner |
| General Characteristics of The relationship | Some initial interest, little is known about each other | Explore each other, begin to set procedures for future contact | Investing more time, energy & effort into each other, mutual understanding & trust begins | Open, honest communications, long term perspective, mutual commitment, win/win approach | Shared vision, complete trust, unity in relationship |
| The Client / Recruit  Characteristics & Behaviors | Shows initial interest in your products / opportunity, heavily influenced by first impressions, Seeks more information, Assesses the representative's character & knowledge,  Seeks the benefit for them & assesses if it's worth investing additional time & effort | Tests the representative and company for the future, Starts to share more information about themselves, commitment is still short-term & low, Draws conclusion as to future direction of relationship | Mutual trust emerges , a sense of commitment begins to develop, Readily shares personal information, dreams, goals, fears etc. | High degree of trust and commitment, starts viewing plans in much longer term perspective, confident and secure in relationship | Complete openness & honesty, long-term perspective, core of relationship is trust & commitment |
| The Financial Representative's Characteristics & Behaviors | Displays a uniqueness  Great first impression  Establishes rapport  Product knowledge expert,  Asks questions, listens  Establishes credibility  Utilizes referrals  Respects boundaries  Honest, high integrity | Explains products and business opportunity  Super service  Keeps commitments  Honest  Under promises – over delivers,  Demonstrates understanding of other persons' needs, wants, dreams  Proves long term intentions & abilities | Proves abilities & keeps promises  Focus on results,  Adds value | Anticipates person's future challenges and needs,  Committed to other person's success,  Long term perspective | Provides real vision based leadership  Totally committed to assist other person be successful, |

**Adapted From Bill Gibson - KBI**

## Networking – A Critical Entrepreneurial Tool

> " The richest people in the world look for and build networks; everyone else looks for work. "
>
> Robert Kiyosaki

Networking is not about meeting as many people as possible and trying to figure out what you can get from them. Rather, it's about making meaningful connections and developing lasting relationships with people. Billionaire Reid Hoffman, co-founder of LinkedIn, has said, "One of the challenges in networking is everybody thinks it's all about making cold calls to strangers. Actually, it's the people who already have strong trust relationships with you, who know you're dedicated, smart, and a team player, who can help you."

When you're an entrepreneur, every chance you get to meet another person is by definition a networking moment. You just never know if the next person you encounter will be a valuable customer, teammate, investor, or even a member of the media that can spread the word about your business. Even if they are not someone that can benefit from your business, they might know someone that could. As you begin to meet various people, make sure that you maintain their contact information and some brief notes about them on your smart phone. That way it's easy to maintain contact with them and, if you are ever are in a position to help them, they are easy to find.

A critical networking tool is the mastering of the "elevator pitch" –a natural sounding speech that describes the essence of your business in matter of seconds. This is a critical skill for many reasons. People normally have a short attention span, so you need to communicate the essence of your business or opportunity within 15 seconds...without sounding frantic! Moreover, in a large networking environment you can't afford to miss many opportunities to connect with others. We highly recommend you develop this skill; practice it, and then take action each and every opportunity you get to use it. Your business will thank you.

A well-crafted elevator speech has three basics components.

1. Explains who you are and outlines what you do.
2. Explains the benefits customers receive from you.
3. Finishes with a call for action - the next step.

Now take a minute to compose and write down your own Elevator Pitch:

_____

_____

A good way to create an elevator introduction is to use the PITCH system (bear in mind that you'll need to vary your approach depending on what your introduction is about and whom you're sharing it with).

**P**urpose – be clear in your mind about the purpose of your introduction.

**I**nspire - start by introducing yourself and describing what you do in an enthusiastic and inspiring way.

**T**arget – explain what problems/challenges your business solves, and who will benefit most from it. Incorporate your USP (unique selling proposition) into the explanation.  What makes your business stand out?

**C**all to Action – do they want to hear more; will they meet for a more detailed discussion?

**H**abit – write down your draft introduction. Make sure that it incorporates the points above. Remove any unnecessary words that don't need to be there. Time yourself rehearsing your introduction to ensure you can give it in 15 seconds or less, using a normal speech rate and remembering to be enthusiastic with your body language, facial expressions and tone of voice. Share it with your coach and teammates, and seek their feedback. Practice your elevator introduction until it becomes a natural habit.

**The following is an example of a well-crafted elevator introduction:**

Purpose – To get feedback on a draft brochure for my at-home wine tasting business, and to inform wine enthusiasts about my business.

**I**nspire – "Hello, my name is Jessica, and I'm launching a new business that combines sampling fine wines with food pairings in the comfort of your own home."

**T**arget – People who, in a comfortable social setting at a friend or colleague's house, learn about great wines not usually available in retail shops while tasting fantastic wines perfectly paired with delicious food.

**C**all to Action – "Would you share about two minutes of your time to give me feedback on my draft brochure?"

**H**abit – Practice this with trusted friends and advisors and seek feedback on how you can improve it.

Use The Space Below to Create Your PITCH

**P**urpose

_____

_____


**I**nspire

_____

_____


**T**arget

_____

_____


**C**all to Action

_____

_____


**H**abit

_____

_____

# Financial Freedom

Now, go back and look at your original Elevator Pitch and see whether it has evolved since you first wrote it. Does it need any more tweaking?

> **Learn to inspire others and you will make millions!**
>
> Bob Graham

We understand that not everyone is an extrovert, and that many people are relatively shy and uncomfortable approaching people they don't know. Taking the initiative to start a conversation with a stranger might seem like a daunting task, but it can be as simple and non-threatening as smiling and saying "Hi!" and then commenting on the weather or the local sports team. Or, try this natural sounding icebreaker: "How's your day going?" The worst thing that can happen is the person will not fully engage with you. But in all likelihood, you will start interesting conversations with most people you approach this way. The key to successful networking is the ability to engage other people in conversations that interest them. To do so, ask lots of questions. As we've said before, the more passionate you are about your business, the easier it will be to come out of your comfort zone in social situations.

> **Life begins at the end of your comfort zone.**
>
> Neale Donald Walsch

# DID YOU KNOW

The Chinese symbol "to listen" is quite complex at first glance. However, once broken down to its four components, it provides insight into what is really involved in active listening.

Ears – I **hear** what you say.

Eyes – I **see** what you say.

Heart – I **feel** what you say.

Undivided Attention – I fully **focus** on you and what you say.

Note: that only one of the four parts is related to the ears, which most people consider the entirety of the listening experience.

## Referrals – The Lifeblood of Every Business

It might be stating the obvious, but your best source of new business is referrals from happy clients. In fact, most of the best recruits come from referrals. Referrals are introductions and recommendations between individuals that have some form of a trusting relationship. The greater the degree of trust, the more impact the referral has. Every business, from professionals such as dentists, lawyers, and financial advisors, to restauranteurs and trade people, benefit from referrals. When business owners learn to tap into the power of referrals, their business will grow quickly.

## How Referable are You and Your Business?

Imagine receiving very poor service and overcooked food at a restaurant. As you pay for your meal, the manager says, "Please accept a free appetizer if you refer your friends to this restaurant." Sadly this is similar to how many companies execute their referral programs. They ask people to refer others to organizations or products that are less than stellar by offering a token referral bonus. It should come as no surprise that this approach to referrals is usually a failure. If you want quality referrals, make sure you deliver on your promises!

Here are the four basic steps to getting lots of glowing referrals.

## Constantly Ask for Referrals

Too many businesspeople forget to ask for referrals. Denis recently asked his real estate agent (who is in the top 1% of all agents), about the best time to ask for a referral. She responded that, from the perspective of a realtor, the best time is within seven days of the close of the home purchase. That's when the agent is still actively involved with the client, and the client is feeling maximum excitement about being in his or her new home.

Don't be shy, either. We have met thousands of people who love the idea of referrals and see their value, but feel that directly asking for them might make them appear desperate or diminish them in a client's eyes. That is totally incorrect. If you deliver great value to your clients and want more people to benefit from your talents, you should be proud and confident to ask, *who else do you know that I could help?*

## Teach Your Clients How to Refer You

Many clients would be happy to refer you, but they simply don't know how. Solve this issue by showing them samples of referrals or testimonials you have already received. You might also simply ask them to pick up the phone to introduce you to a friend or colleague. The call might consist of no more than a brief description of the service or product you provided, and that the friend or colleague might also benefit from a meeting with you.

## Mobile Tip

Have an easy to read, natural sounding script on your mobile phone that can be texted to, or even read by your client as a referral.

## Remind Them to Refer You

It is a great practice to keep in touch with current and past clients and, occasionally, to ask for referrals from old clients. Denis' real estate agent sends out a quarterly electronic newsletter that updates market issues, adds some personal interest material and, in every issue, reminds readers that she appreciates their support and loves referrals. She freely admits in each newsletter that referrals are the lifeblood of her business. This is a real motivator for Denis, because she did such a good job selling his last house that he wants to help her!

## Say "Thank You," and Do it Often

Anyone who gives you a referral has given you a great gift. First of all, thank the person. Secondly, honor them and the gift by quickly following up on the referral. Reward the referrer with a genuine gesture of thanks – e.g., a gift certificate at a nice restaurant, or a free book. Keep the gift simple, relatively inexpensive, and relevant to the size and number of referrals. Also make sure that the gift does not break any rules that might constrain your profession or industry. Remember: most referrers are motivated to help you because you helped them, and are not seeking a reward themselves.

Generating referrals is not hard work once you have developed the habit. And you can be sure that this is one habit that will make your business much more successful.

# Financial Freedom

## Recruiting GREAT People

Any expanding business needs more people. The best way to get more people is to seek them out. This is called recruiting. Employers of choice – that is to say, companies with exceptional reputations like Google or Apple - one of the most coveted positions is to be one of their recruiters. A recruiter's job is to seek out the best people to join their successful team – and they get paid to do this! Successful entrepreneurs need to have their recruiting radar on 24/7 because you never know what random event will lead you to a superstar teammate.

When recruiting, remember that prospective recruits are buying into you as much as your business. While you are assessing their fit in terms of skills, knowledge, attitudes and aspirations, they are assessing you in the same way. While every recruiter responds to a positive, confident, goal-driven candidate, some recruiters fail to realize the importance of their behaving the same way, and especially of projecting the rare value of membership on their own team. So when you act as your own recruiter, remember to share your vision of the future, being sure to show how the business can fulfill the goals and dreams of the recruit. Finally, never forget that it's always better to recruit for **Attitude** and **Ambition** and then train for **Competence** and **Skills**.

> ## Your "I Can" is more important than your "IQ."
>
> Robin Sharma

The challenge with the traditional methods most companies use in recruiting is that they were designed for the last century. As we already mentioned, the nature of business has greatly changed. Disruptors (near and offshore) are requiring business owners and the people they attract to their business to be more productive, innovative, entrepreneurial and agile in today's ever-changing corporate landscape. Whether you are looking for a new employee, a free-lancer, a sub-contractor or a business associate, you will need to be aware of how to attract, recruit and retain great people. We will discuss additional topics relating to retaining people later in this section.

## DID YOU KNOW

From a recruiting perspective, GREAT recruits for a 21st century business are:

**G**oal oriented, with a burning desire to win;

**R**eputable, with high moral standards and integrity;

**E**nthusiastic about self-development and the opportunity to be part of a team; having an

**A**ttitude of positive professionalism; and the

**T**enacity to "do it" until the job gets done.

Unfortunately, there is no proven test to assess how GREAT a person is, so most organizations don't bother investing much energy into this part of the process. By default, they focus virtually all of their efforts on the more traditional elements. Conventional thinking favors a candidate with an MBA, 20+ years of experience and an IQ of 162 or higher. We contend that such thinking is fatally flawed. If this "ideal" candidate also has a history of blaming others for their shortcomings, a pervasive negative attitude, and a lack of initiative and ambition, they would likely be a poor performer and might in fact poison the attitude of any team that includes them. Contrast that individual with someone of average credentials and abilities, but who is also coachable and has a burning desire to win. That's the kind of person we would try to entice to our team!

Traditional recruiting usually entails some form of paid message – newspaper ads, messages on virtual job boards, booths at a career fairs, help wanted signs, recruiting messages on cash register receipts, messages on LinkedIn, ads on such online recruiting portals as Monster and Workopolis, and so on. Recruiting messages are everywhere! If the message is compelling, the recruiter can easily be overwhelmed by applications, and the first job is to pare down the number to a manageable size. The screening process normally consists of a cursory review of the applicant's resume, a process which does nothing to assess character, ambition, tenacity, values, or the competitive nature of the candidate. As we have already emphasized, these are the very qualities that are most correlated with success in the new economy.

The one traditional recruiting approach that is still 100% relevant is word of mouth referrals. Savvy businesses have long recognized the value of an endorsement from a trusted teammate or employee. In fact, many of the world's most successful companies have formalized employee referral programs such that referring employees are often awarded substantial amounts of money when they endorse a candidate who is hired and successfully completes the probationary period. This thinking makes sense because your most successful people are those who are most likely to associate with other like-minded, successful people. Moreover, your own best teammates care about the success of the business and, as solid team members, they understand the importance of referring someone to a venture that affects their own career directly.

We are not suggesting that social media and other methods aren't useful in creating an awareness of your business and it's opportunities, but nothing beats the power of a referral. When connecting with a recruit, it is okay for the first point of contact to occur via text, email or social media. But the more substantive parts of the recruitment process require a face-to-face meeting between both parties.

Another major flaw in traditional recruiting is the notion that the recruit has to go to the HR office for a traditional interview. With people telecommuting, working flex hours, doing trans-border business, and conducting so much business in coffee shops and other non-corporate venues, it's only appropriate that a recruiting interview be as likely to occur in a coffee shop or a home office as a typical HR suite in a corporate office building. Moreover, traditional HR professionals- particularly in large corporations - can be so removed from the specific job to be filled that they are ill-equipped to assess an applicant's real qualifications. Indeed, how can they assess someone's potential to do a job they have never done? Yes, we believe an interviewer must assess the potential of the applicant, as well as how well they might mesh with the corporate culture (which is unique to every business). But it is also important that the interviewer showcase and explain the opportunities that the company has to offer. Consider this: if the recruit is so good, aren't they just as likely to be considering other opportunities? The interview is the perfect opportunity for both parties to promote their value to the other.

The final point we want to make is that you should not wait for a specific opening to start recruiting. Rather, imitate the really successful entrepreneurs, who have their recruiting radars turned on 24/7. That is to say, always be on the look-out for GREAT people to strengthen your growing team.

## The Four Step Recruiting Process

### Step 1: Maintain a professional and positive sense of urgency.
Like-minded people attract each other. Because today's economy forces business owners to be positive, professional, and results oriented, recruiters who clearly embody these qualities will attract recruits with similar characteristics. If you give the clear impression that you're doing something important at the beginning of every telephone call or interview, your initial point of contact will be shorter, there will be fewer questions, and both parties will have a higher respect for each other and their time.

The role of the initial point of contact is to develop rapport, get a quick read of each other, and confirm the time and location for a more in-depth interview. The prospective recruit should, in one way or another, be told that, "I know we are both very busy people but it's great to connect over a quick coffee." The point is not to memorize and reel off some pre-arranged script but, in your own words, to say something appropriate to facilitate a quick, casual, initial chat.

### Step 2: Focus on the positive attributes of the recruit. If you have
identified a GREAT potential recruit, show it, and offer them a sincere compliment (NOTE: the compliment must be sincere). A perceptive compliment can open the door to an insightful interview. Candidates who feel appreciated and at ease are much more likely to open up about their dreams, ambitions, values, and work ethics. Such candidates are also much more likely to hear what you have to say about your own company and corporate culture. Under appropriate conditions, the following should be said to a potential recruit:

"You've been very successful in many different roles, and that's the type of person I'm looking for on my team."

"You're one of the most positive and energetic people I've ever met, and it shows in the caliber of people you are connected to."

"You have a sharp business mind, and can see the bigger picture that others often don't see."

**Step 3: Ask a compelling question and provide proof of your statements.** This step comprises two elements: asking a compelling question to capture interest and weed out misfits, and providing proof of the claims you are about to make. The following are things that might be said to a prospective recruit:

"Let me ask you a serious question: if there was a business in which you could start off working part-time, that would eventually lead to full-time income, would that interest you?"

"With your work ethic, skills, and contacts, and our proven training system, you could make significant money in a business I've recently started."

"I work with a company that's expanding in our area, and I'm looking for some sharp people who are interested in additional cash flow. Do you know anyone who might fit that description?"

If the above questions incite interest in the other person, that's great. They will naturally have some follow-up questions of their own, which is great because it shows their interest. In light of the fact that this is just an initial chat, and you both are busy people, be respectful of each other's time and move on to the next step.

Remember, not everyone will fully understand how they might fit in with the potential opportunities that might grow out of the position you're trying to fill. By nature, many people are very skeptical of initial claims made by those who don't already have massive and self-evident credibility. Your business might involve new technology, a unique marketing approach, or a critical element of an emerging industry. You might be one of those disruptors we mentioned in the first section. But remember; wild exaggerations will ultimately backfire, so be sure the statements you make about growth potential are plausible and/or demonstrably defensible. Be prepared to provide additional evidence to support any especially glowing comments you make about the growth of your business and how the right person could benefit from it. The best way to do this is through the use of any available, credible third party tools, such as a blog by a well-known, respected Thought Leader; a profile of someone who has been very successful in a similar business; a research paper showing a growing, long-term demand for your product or services; client testimonial videos or letters; or books that reinforce your arguments. The following is an illustration of ways in which you might present this kind of corroborating evidence:

"If I gave you a DVD that laid out all the information in a very professional way, would you watch it?"

"I can see a healthy skepticism in your eyes. I don't blame you; I felt the same way. So I came prepared with this book published this year. All I ask is that you read it over and then get back to me."

**Step 4: Set and confirm the next meeting.** Once you feel a candidate shows some potential as a future teammate,and once they've shown an interest in your business, it's time to set up a more formal interview. Once a time and place has been agreed upon, politely suggest that they put this appointment in a place they won't forget it. While saying this, you can be updating your calendar on your mobile and, by doing so, sending the message that you are taking this meeting seriously. Finally, make sure you get the best number to reach them should there be any last minute scheduling changes. Remember, you are both busy people, so the worst thing to do is to keep on talking and selling your business to the other person. Both parties will have lots of time to explore things in depth during the next meeting. The best thing is to say something like: "Great! I look forward to talking with you more then. Gotta run!"

## Retention: The Art of Keeping GREAT People

> **If you help others get what they want, they will help you get what you want.**
>
> ZigZiglar

The retention of GREAT people is critical to sustaining your business. It's not enough to be an effective recruiter; you need to hang on to those great people that you invested so much time and effort in training and developing. Note, we are not suggesting that 100% retention should be the goal. Such leading companies as Apple, Google and Tesla, to name just a few, pay their people very well, have great brands, and invest heavily in the professional development of their staff. Still, some of their people do leave. The point is to minimize the loss of good people. If your community comes to see your business as a place that can't retain people, it will greatly impact your brand. The best starting point in retaining your best people is to be a dynamic, deserving leader yourself.

Our definition of leadership is, "the ability to turn a dream or a vision into reality with the support and assistance of other people, while helping them achieve their own dreams."

Remember, you can't demand respect from your team. It has to be earned over time. Another way to look at leadership is to compare it to gardening. Gardeners use sunlight, water, fertilizer and good soil to turn seeds into wonderful plants. Leaders use communication, self-esteem, vision, recognition, friendly competition, rewards and their own personal and organizational goals to help their team reach its potential. Business leaders, then, can be seen as the gardeners of corporate America.

Before going any further there are six commonly accepted myths of leadership that we want to dispel.

## Leadership Myth Number 1: Leadership is a Rare Skill

We, the ABC Guys, don't think leadership ability is rare. In fact, as you look around, you see all sorts of day-to-day examples of great leadership in action. For example, you can go to your local gym and see dozens of parents volunteering their time to be coaches. Coaches, most definitely, are leaders. They put on their leadership cap after work, on weekends, in the wee hours of the morning – any time they can escape their overflowing schedules. You see it on baseball fields, swimming pools, arenas, and dance halls. Of course, people volunteer for leadership roles over a range of contexts infinitely wider than sports. From the presidency of the local Lion's Club to the Chairman of the Board of a global anti-cancer organization, you'll find an abundance of positions that presuppose leadership skills.

Putting vocational skills to work in our personal life is something we all can relate to. The challenge is to remember that this also works in reverse, and to use the leadership skills we have developed on our own time in our own business.

## Leadership Myth Number 2: Leaders are Born

Another common leadership myth is that leaders are born, not made. But leadership actually is the result of an interaction between your life experiences and "reference groups." Reference groups are a critical part of the human environment; they include people like our parents, siblings, and friends, as well as institutions such as educational systems, religious organizations, and the mass media. Our reference groups become a critical part of our environment. The person we become, including whether we grow up to be a leader or a follower, result from our reaction to things we're exposed to at a young age and how they are explained by our reference groups. Leaders are not born; rather, they are created as a result of their experiences and their expectations, as well as what they've learned from their reference groups.

## Leadership Myth Number 3: Leadership is the Same Thing as Management

Managers attempt to do things right — that is, they do what is required according to rules, policies, regulations, and systems — whereas leaders try to do the right things. We see management as the day-to-day supervision of the systems and the people of an organization. Leaders, on the other hand, have the ability to help teammates reach their potential, even in the face of the teammate's fear and self-doubt, and then getting all the players to work together as a cohesive team.

## Leadership Myth Number 4: Leadership Only Exists at the Top

It is completely wrong to claim that leadership only exists at the top of an organization. Sometimes top leadership is very lean, but there is strong leadership throughout the body of the organization. Consider, for example, a shop steward who represents a union. This person might be sitting at the bottom of the actual hierarchical chart of the organization, but he or she has real and legitimate power, as well as a bona-fide leadership role. There are leaders within departments, leaders within divisions, leaders within work groups, and leaders working on various projects within an organization. So, we believe that leadership is not a function of someone sitting on top of the corporate totem pole; rather, leadership is the habit of making a conscious decision to take an active role to bring value to others and the organization.

> Humility recognizes that the only master there is on earth is a servant. All those who seek the power and the glory of the title "master" will fail. The servant works twenty hours a day while others are sleeping and enjoying holidays, and through their hard work becomes the master.
>
> Bill Gibson

## Leadership Myth Number 5: Leadership Power is a Bad Thing

The power that attends leadership is neither good or bad per se; it's your intentions as a leader that lead to positive or negative results. If you have honorable intentions, and if you are sincerely trying to do positive things within the organization, then we consider your power to be positive. But if you use your power for personal enrichment at the expensive of others, or to execute a hostile takeover of a corporation, then we consider your power to be a negative force.

As we have said, leadership power is not intrinsically selfish or evil. Quite the contrary. In fact, we recommend that as a leader you deliberately try to expand your leadership power base. Isn't leadership power ultimately the ability to influence others? As a leader, power is the ability to motivate the entire team to come on board and share a common vision.

> **He who thinks he leads, but has no followers, is only taking a walk.**
>
> John Maxwell

The best way to understand how to obtain more influence is to review the Five Levels of Leadership, an idea developed by John Maxwell in his great books on leadership. The lowest level of leadership, which also has the least amount of influence, is based on position. That is to say, the person's job title implies or requires the ability to influence. The reality is that influence is earned, as can be seen in the list below. This list summarizes Maxwell's hierarchy of leadership types, ranging from 1-5 in order of increasing levels of leadership ability.

**Level 5: Purpose** – Vision based, founded on the principles you stand for. If you don't stand for something, you will fall for anything.

**Level 4: Progress** – You have mentored others and helped them progress in career and life.

**Level 3: Peer** – You treat teammates as equals.

**Level 2: Performance** – You are judged by your results, not your words.

**Level 1: Position** – The job title means virtually nothing without the above.

# Myth Number 6: Leaders are Created Only by Extraordinary Events

There is no need for a shocking or traumatic event to propel someone into a position of leadership, although this kind of thing certainly has happened. There are in fact many unsung heroes, day-to-day leaders who weren't catapulted into their position. On the contrary, the more common type of leader is driven by a daily dissatisfaction with the way certain industries or organizations are run. Moreover, they are ambitious and/or courageous enough to do something about it. As a result, they take a road that naturally leads them to the top, and leadership comes to them. Leaders require the confidence to call the shots. Even when they fail they must have the wisdom to learn from their mistakes.

> **Find the lesson in every failure and you'll never fail.**
>
> Unknown

## Success Habits

- Be an early riser
- Be early for all appointments
- Be visionary and engage your people
- Develop others so that your business can run without you
- Know your daily disciplines and commit to doing them every day.
- Replace bad habits with good habits.

## Recognition: Acknowledging Great Work and Effort

Providing recognition to a deserving colleague is one of the most powerful tools any company or leader can use to motivate teammates and stimulate growth, productivity and sales. But even though special recognition strengthens loyalty and builds relationships, corporate engagement surveys consistently show that most employees do not feel recognized for their efforts. Some companies spend lavishly on annual holiday parties for their staff. Such gestures are nice, and they are appreciated, but their impact is diluted by their impersonality. Genuine recognition – it must be genuine – can have more impact than the most expensive party. The recognition can be very inexpensive; in fact, often times there is no need for it to cost anything but a few well-chosen minutes. A few points to consider:

1. Recognize contributions by good team members and not just your top producers. Many people work quietly in the background and manage to meet all of their goals and deadlines. That sort of quiet competence certainly deserves recognition.

2. Recognize – and reinforce – the skill you most want to develop in someone. You might, for instance, want to reward the ability of a customer service representative to smile through a stressful encounter. For someone not noted for their ability to stay on task, it might be wise to celebrate an instance of their organizing and planning a significant event or project. Yet others, who are blessed with creativity (or cursed by the lack of it), would be energized by public recognition of a brilliant insight they had that solved a particularly important problem.

3. For your top producers, a private lunch out of the office is a nice acknowledgment and reward, but formally recognizing your top people in front of the entire team is much more powerful. Organize a monthly or quarterly meeting of all the staff or teammates, and start off with a few words about how the company is doing and where it's headed. Then give out the weekly or monthly achievement awards: who was the top producer over the period? Who was second and third? Which employee was the best at providing customer service? Which employee brought the most value to the company in that period? The prizes can range from an inscribed plaque or a $10 gift certificate to a trip for two to a vacation resort. Investing in your teammates will reap incredible rewards because it creates an atmosphere of friendly competition and stimulates other teammates to push harder to achieve recognition the next time.

# Financial Freedom

## Replication of Others through Coaching

> **The chief responsibility of a leader: To engage your people by coaching them and turn each teammate's talent into performance during times of change and uncertainty.**
>
> Marcus Buckingham

Most companies focus on training their people to do things better, whereas the most progressive organizations develop their people to be better. We want to be clear that we are not against training; in fact, there can be a tremendous value in sharpening skills and increasing knowledge. What we are saying is that development is more holistic in nature because its purpose is to assist an individual realize his or her unique potential. This is true whether you're managing a small retail or service shop, or a billion dollar corporation.

When developing future leaders, we suggest that you consider using the characteristics of the Entrepreneurial Assessment in the first section as guide for mentoring and grooming future leaders.

The most obvious reason for developing your people is to help them achieve their potential, while equipping them to provide the maximum benefit to your organization and themselves and their loved ones. In order for team development to occur, you need two key elements: a leader who will act as a coach while creating a positive learning environment, and an individual or group of leadership candidates who are "coachable." A coachable person is enthusiastic about developing himself or herself, and is prepared to step out of their comfort zone and in order to learn new things.

> **Your life doesn't get better by chance; it gets better by change.**
>
> Jim Rohn

Coaching, sometimes referred to as mentoring, is similar to teaching except that a coach has a deeper relationship with the learner. A coach cares about a teammate's long term success, and is committed to help "fast-track" the trainee's development. Much of the actual coaching consists of a real time sharing of the coach's own hard-won lessons on-the-job. This form of compressed learning can literally shave off many years of development for a new teammate.

The following diagram, adapted from the work of Jack Welch and his senior team at GE,is a powerful tool to assess both the current and potential performance of your people.

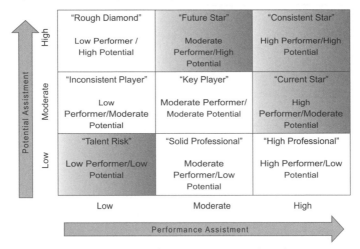

Figure1. Current and potential performance potential analysis as conceived by Jack Welch at General Electric.

By helping your people become more skilled, you bring value to them and your business. A great model that illustrates the process of going from unskilled to highly skilled in a specific area is by Abraham Maslow's Four Levels of Learning. Your role as a coach is to guide your people through each of the following phases.

1. The first phase is the "ignorance is bliss" phase, in which your protégés are totally unaware of their lack of skill. As a coach, you want your charges to move out of this phase as quickly as possible.

2. In the second phase, your protégés are shown just how unskilled they actually are. This phase is critical because it shows their

willingness to step beyond their comfort zone. If the revelation of their current degree of incompetence is too embarrassing, they will resist taking on anything more challenging. But if they are shown their need of the developmental opportunities you can offer, and if this happens in a supportive and non-threatening way, they are more likely to embrace your message and example.

3. The third phase can be a dangerous trap if someone stays there too long. This is the phase in which people suffer from the "know-it-all" syndrome. As a coach, you must ensure that neither you nor your charges get stuck here.

4. The final phase is ideal from the perspective of personal development. In this phase, our protégés realize that, despite their obvious knowledge and skills, they still have things to learn. Thus they remain open to continuous learning and to coaching even after having attained a considerable degree of mastery.

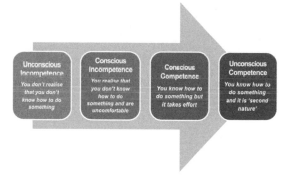

Figure1. Current and potential performance potential analysis as conceived by Jack Welch at General Electric.

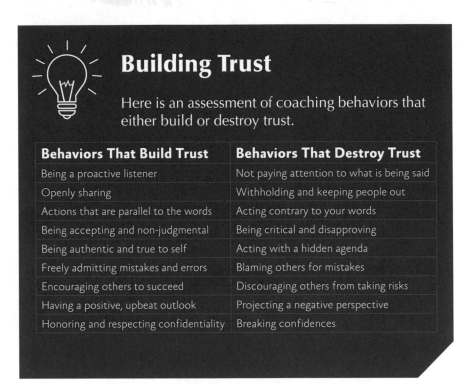

## Building Trust

Here is an assessment of coaching behaviors that either build or destroy trust.

| Behaviors That Build Trust | Behaviors That Destroy Trust |
| --- | --- |
| Being a proactive listener | Not paying attention to what is being said |
| Openly sharing | Withholding and keeping people out |
| Actions that are parallel to the words | Acting contrary to your words |
| Being accepting and non-judgmental | Being critical and disapproving |
| Being authentic and true to self | Acting with a hidden agenda |
| Freely admitting mistakes and errors | Blaming others for mistakes |
| Encouraging others to succeed | Discouraging others from taking risks |
| Having a positive, upbeat outlook | Projecting a negative perspective |
| Honoring and respecting confidentiality | Breaking confidences |

At this point we hope that your plan for achieving Financial Freedom has come into sharper focus. You should also have a better handle on your personal finances, and a better idea of how to finance your new venture. You probably also have a better appreciation for the importance of being able to communicate your ideas clearly and comfortably with the people whose support you will need – teammates, suppliers and customers. Successful business owners positively enjoy managing and maintaining these relationships and especially in helping their teammates accomplish great things for the business and themselves.

# Financial Freedom

## Section Three: Creating Your Financial Freedom

As we said in the first section, the safety and security of the "job for life" is a relic from a bygone age, alongside the abacus and the typewriter. As we speed toward 2020, more and more traditional businesses will fall victim to the Disruptors. Thus it is vital that the modern business owner be quick and agile in order to avoid being left on the scrap heap of history. Remember, some of the biggest disruptors – now worth billions of dollars –didn't exist ten years ago. Moreover, some of the current movers and shakers will be completely forgotten ten years from now. That's the nature of disruptors and the reality of business as we approach 2020.

## Examples of Some Key Disruptors

### APPLE

Long known for their superior computer architecture and design, Apple re-imagined the way music is bought, stored and played. In 2001 they gave us the iPod, which has sold about400 million units. They also supported the iPod with the iTunes organization system, which allowed people to legally download music and take it with them anywhere they wanted to go. It cut music piracy in half, restored lost revenue to musicians, and virtually eliminated all other players in the sector.

In 2007, they combined a computer, web browser, music and video storage system, and a camera, into a unit that fit comfortably in your hand. They called it the iPhone. (Oh yeah: iPhones can also be used to make phone calls). They also created a whole new industry for Apps which now generates billions of dollars for App creators and Apple. Blackberry's head is still spinning.

### NETFLIX

Remember going to a video store like Blockbuster and looking at rack after rack of movie titles, picking one and then hoping you'd remember to get it back before the late charges kicked in? When Netflix made their movies available online, it was revolutionary because it eliminated the need to go somewhere to get or return your video. And to be able to choose whatever you want, any time you want, and to watch as much as you want, all for one fairly low monthly fee – a totally brilliant idea. Then Netflix started to commission their own series and movies, underwritten by large budgets. The result: buzz worthy, award-winning programming. Again, quality rules. Blockbuster, not so much.

## TESLA

No one ever accused Elon Musk of being a small thinker. Sure, electric cars were around 100 years ago, before being displaced by the internal combustion engine. GM had a model in the 1980s, but shelved the idea while it was still being tested. Musk came along with a luxury electric car that produced a great range and was fun to drive, but he didn't stop there. He poured money into infrastructure (Charging stations) and battery storage, reducing the size and cost. Now you can buy a home power storage unit called the Powerwall. He also owns the largest solar panel company (SolarCity) in America. Thus, you can collect the sun's energy, store it and use it in your house and your car, all courtesy of one visionary leader. And we haven't even mentioned Space X or his high speed transportation idea known as the Hyperloop.

## UBER

Until recently, taxis and airport limousines paid cities up to $300,000 for licenses that gave them the right to pick up and deliver passengers. Then Uber showed up with an app that made it easy to connect with a nearby driver who would, in most cases, be driving a better car than the typical taxi, and which would get you to your destination for less than the cost of a taxi. This was done without the need for a tip, and it was all transacted on your credit card, eliminating the need for cash or any paperwork at the end of the journey.

## Airbnb

Hotels are great - a home away from home. But, they can be a little impersonal, pricey, sometimes charge silly prices for their food and beverages, and don't even think about opening the in-room fridge. Well, there's an app for that now. Airbnb allows anyone with a spare room, apartment or house to make it available for rent, usually at a better rate than a major hotel. Sometimes it's a shared room with the owner, sometimes it's fully self-contained. Rooms are often in residential areas, making for a "homier" travel experience. Moreover, at this point in time, there are no additional taxes or fees tacked on at the end of your stay. Airbnb and Uber have completely disrupted the hotel and taxi industries.

## LinkedIn

From its early days as a helpful networking site for business people, LinkedIn has expanded to become a crucial part of recruiting and professional job searching. Whether you're trying to find a connection with someone at a company you're hoping to join, or a recruiter searching for someone with the right qualifications, this is a value tool that has rewritten the way people seek and get jobs.

## Pros and Cons of Different Business Structures

### Start from Scratch

When starting a business from scratch, you can build your dream from the ground up based only on turning your interests into reality.

**PROS:** You get to focus on what you're passionate about and then apply it to building your dream business. So, if you love coffee, you open up a really homey space filled with comfortable chairs and sofas, great decorations and a fantastic selection of music to set the tone. You take all the money you've saved, then borrow money from family and friends, build great relationships with ethical suppliers sourcing only fair-trade beans, and cultivate a team of creative baristas who are as passionate about the most popular drink in the world as you. The customers love the ambiance and service, and in no time you've got a loyal clientele. Great; you've achieved your dream! Or have you? What do you do when a Starbucks opens up across the street?

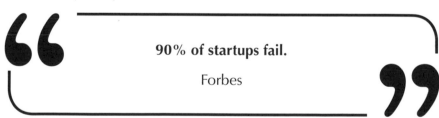

**90% of startups fail.**

Forbes

**CONS:** According to the Kauffman Foundation new ventures are more likely to fail than they are to succeed. Starting a new business from scratch can seem overwhelming. Questions such as what to start, where to start and how to start your business can plague you and rob you of your ability to sleep. Gone is the notion of the 40-hour work week; as a business owner trying to get a new company off the ground, your schedule of "half-days" translates to 12 hours a day, seven days a week. You will either have to master wearing many hats or you will need to hire people and dilute your equity by bringing on partners. All tasks, big or small, need your attention: hiring and firing employees, arranging contracts and securing suppliers, raising funds, getting clients, and performing less glamorous jobs, like cleaning. Then there is the unexpected, like a franchise moving in nearby and taking your business; or there's a strike and you can't access goods from your supplier; or someone gets sick and takes to social media to blame it on your food with absolutely no supporting evidence. Things like this are unpredictable, sometimes very unfair, and there's little you can do to prepare for them.

## Buy an Existing Business

Buying an established business with a proven track record can be a viable option for many would be entrepreneurs.

**PROS:** Generally revolve around a reduced exposure to risk compared to a startup. Buying a successful business is less risky than starting your own business, especially if you can afford a business that is already well managed and profitable. The previous owner survived the difficult start-up phase and is established in the marketplace with loyal customers, contractors, suppliers, and staff, as well as proven a location, equipment and inventory that have stood the test of time.

**CONS:** Generally relate to the difficulty of discriminating fact from fiction in the sales pitch. Consider your mother's tried and true advice: If it seems too good to be true, it probably is. Not every business on the market is a good venture. Many owners want to bail out of unprofitable or under-performing businesses. Consider for a moment: if you risked everything and invested 20 years of your life in building a well-oiled money making machine, would you sell it cheap? Of course not. The seller is likely retiring and needs to get every possible dollar from the sales price. Another concept to consider when buying an existing business is the "Goodwill" that has become associated with it. Goodwill is an accounting term that refers to the intangible value of the owner's good name (brand) and his or her personal connection with the business (loyal clients, trusted suppliers and a host of other professional relationships tied to the owner, but not to the actual business). Therefore, a new owner should expect to pays tens - if not hundreds - of thousands of additional dollars for goodwill that, unfortunately, begins to evaporate the moment the former owner steps out the door. The reality is that any existing business worth having will command a hefty price tag, one that most people simply can't pay. And even if a new owner can come up with the goodwill surcharge, there's no guarantee that the customers or suppliers will honor the deal and treat you as they used to treat the founder.

# Financial Freedom

## Invest in a Franchise

Can people make money by investing in a franchise system? There are many examples of profitable franchise systems to be found. In fact the number one reason people invest in a franchise is because of a proven business system and brand.

**PROS:** One of the major Pros of buying into a franchise is the opportunity to sell an established product or service, usually with brand-name recognition. This gives the franchisee the benefits of a pre-sold customer base that would ordinarily take years to establish. A franchise increases the odds of business success because of proven products and methods. Franchises offer important pre-opening support, too: site selection, design, construction, financing, training, a grand-opening program plus advertising and ongoing operational support.

**CONS:** The negatives of investing in a franchise are mostly associated with the constraints the franchise imposes on the franchisee and on the ways the business can be operated. Sadly, most franchise agreements are so restrictive that many conventional jobs seem to provide more operational freedom than owning a franchise. The franchisee's agreement spells out all of the procedures and operational restrictions which include acceptable uniforms, mandatory hours of operations, and exclusive suppliers – even if you can get many items more cheaply elsewhere. Typical franchise agreements do not, however, stop with uniforms and hours and suppliers; they also cover which products or services can be offered, pricing, and geographic territory limits. Moreover, franchisees must pay ongoing royalties and advertising fees in addition to the initial steep franchise owner fee. Agreements are confusing and very lengthy in order to protect the franchisor, not the franchisee. The term (duration) of a franchise agreement is usually limited and the franchisee may have little or nothing to say about the causes for termination, or even if their children can take over the business, because the franchisor has final vetting authority.

The powerlessness of the franchisee in worth reiterating. Few elements of the franchise agreement actually protect the franchisee. If the franchisor wants to sell to another franchisee that wants to locate a block away from your store, they have the right to do so. Never forget that the franchisor is not in business to make you rich. Moreover, when stuff hits the fan in the head office, the franchisees feel it first. If the board decides to enter into a sale or partnership with another corporation, and that venture turns sour, the whole franchise machine can run off the tracks. That can ruin the name of the franchise and force them to raise all their fees to the franchisee to bail them out of problems that were no fault of the franchisees.

# DID YOU KNOW

Every year Entrepreneur Magazine publishes its list of the top 500 franchises in North America. We have their current top ten and the initial investment required for each. As you can see, not many ordinary people can afford to raise this kind of money!

| Name | 2017 Ranking | Cost |
|---|---|---|
| Seven-Eleven | 1 | $37,000 to $1,600,000 |
| McDonald's | 2 | $1,000,000 to $2,000,000 |
| Dunkin Donuts | 3 | $229,000 to $1,700,000 |
| UPS Store | 4 | $159,000 to $435,000 |
| Jimmy John's | 5 | $326,000 to $555,000 |
| Dairy Queen | 6 | $361,000 to 1,800,000 |
| Ace Hardware | 7 | $273,000 to 1,600,000 |
| Wingsstop | 8 | $303,000 to $923,000 |
| Sport clips | 9 | $183,000 to$352,000 |
| RE/Max | 10 | $380,000 to $524,000 |

## Direct Marketing Companies

Direct Marketing companies have been around for decades. They offer individuals the opportunity to quickly get into an existing business. The reality is that Direct Marketing companies run the range from illegal pyramid schemes to sound businesses.

**PROS:** Direct Marketing companies are often referred to as "Network Marketing Companies," because one of the best things about this industry is its reliance on word-of-mouth referrals and introductions via a network of personal contacts. As we said earlier, referrals and word-of-mouth are the best ways to grow a reputable business, and this model really relies on that principle. Because one's network is ingrained into the business structure, these businesses have explosive growth potential.

**CONS:** The flip side of relying on one's network is if the company, its products or services are flawed in some way, then people wind up burning through family, friends and other connections to the point of ruining some relationships. The companies to avoid are the ones that rely on **internal consumption**. That is, any company that insists on you buying - they'll call it "investing in" – thousands, and in some cases tens of thousands of dollars worth of their products, and then getting you to convince other people to do the same thing. The challenge is for anyone to actually sell these "pills, potions and lotions" to people outside the company. No matter how much better a company claims their products to be, if you can buy a similar product for a much lower price at a place like Wal-Mart, most people will. You're then stuck with expensive inventory that you'll end up throwing in the garbage in a fit of despair. Not surprisingly, over 90% of Direct Marketing companies go out of business within a few years. Our advice: stay away from those opportunities, regardless of the financial promises they make.

# 20/20 Vision of the Perfect Business

With such a wide array of businesses available, we are constantly asked by would-be entrepreneurs for guidance in selecting the best business opportunities for them. For almost two decades we have shared our "15 Power Points of the Ideal Business." This tool has helped tens of thousands of entrepreneurs consider the pros and cons when assessing the potential of any business idea.

As the year 2020 approaches, we have decided to update this list of criteria for the perfect business. As we mentioned earlier in this section, various Disruptors have already impacted virtually every industry, or are on the verge of doing so. We felt that it was essential to modernize and refine our list. The list on the following page details the **20 Points of The Perfect Business For The Year 2020 and Beyond**. The greater the number of these points that your business model addresses directly, the greater its **potential for success today and well beyond 2020!**

Please take the time to analyze each business you are considering starting or joining using the work form below. The last row, labeled **Score out of 20**, refers to the 20 points of The Perfect Business summarized on the next page.

| Business Opportunity: |
| --- |
| Overview of business opportunity:<br><br>Pros:<br><br>Cons:<br><br><br> |
| **Score out of 20:** |

By analyzing various business opportunities with this approach, you will answer one of the most fundamental of all business questions: **Is this business opportunity for real?** By determining, for instance, that a particular business ranks high in the 20-point system on the next page, you are well on your way to finding the best business for you. Now take the time to review the highest scoring business and then ask yourself these last three critical questions as they apply to this business:

1. Have other people like me been successful in this type of business?
2. Are there people and systems in place to help me succeed in this business?
3. Are there any assurances of success that accompany this business?

# The Perfect Business

The Perfect Business Opportunity for the year 2020 and beyond should have as many of the 20 qualities in the list below as possible.

1.  Does the business sell to the masses?
2.  Does it meet a fundamental need for most people?
3.  Is it low risk?
4.  Does it provide an opportunity for passive income?
5.  Does it have a low staffing requirement?
6.  Does it have a stable, growing, long-term demand?
7.  Does it have low overhead costs?
8.  Does it have low startup costs?
9.  Are its products, services or business practices unique, thus providing a strategic advantage?
10. Does it have positive cash flow and low inventory costs?
11. Does it have a high profit margin and/or rate of return?
12. Does it have systems to simplify compliance with all regulations?
13. Is it portable?
14. Is it fun, challenging and satisfying for the business owner?
15. Does it leverage technology while maintaining face-to-face relationships?
16. Does it use "word of mouth" referrals primarily, avoiding expensive paid advertising?
17. Does it have a system designed for massive distribution?
18. Does it have a track record of providing thousands of ordinary people six figure plus incomes?
19. Does it have a proven coaching system that fast-tracks people's rate of success?
20. Does it provide an opportunity to discover other money-making businesses?

# Financial Freedom

Over the years we examined well over a thousand business opportunities. Almost all scored very low our on our original 15 point scale, and even worse on our revised 20 point scale. A very small number initially held some promise but, due to the greed of the founders, or fundamental design flaws in their structure or system, or the dependence on internal consumption, they fell short after detailed scrutiny. We have analyzed pills, potions and lotions, travel, diet and fitness, household goods, jewelry, and telecommunications, as well business networking and dozens of other categories. **The fact remains that there is only one business that we have found with the vision and viability for the year 2020 and beyond, and scores a perfect 20 out of 20.** As researchers we have tried for years to find the flaw or limitations in the Primerica business opportunity but, in all honesty, we have yet to find any.

Primerica is a financial services distribution powerhouse with approximately 120,000 representatives in The United States and Canada. This debt free company's stock is listed on the New York Stock Exchange (PRI). It has a 40-year track record of positively impacting the middle class. Just like us, the company's philosophy has been to educate their clients to buy more affordable term life insurance and invest the difference.

Primerica also scores points when it comes to setting up the perfect business, with very low startup costs, low overhead costs, and a high and stable long term growth potential. It's not uncommon for part timers to earn an extra $1,000 or more a month. If the opportunity does not work out for someone, then that's because they did not invest enough time and effort into the business. With a market penetration currently less than 3%, and a growing need for their products and services, the growth potential for 2020 and beyond is massive.

Our feeling has always been that there is no downside to joining the company because at the very least new members receive a fantastic financial education for an incredibly low investment. If they simply apply those lessons learned they would be well on their way to Financial Freedom.

We have re-examined our findings on Primerica several times over the years and always come to the same positive conclusion. Surprisingly, we still get comments from people who suggest that this is a pyramid scheme. We know what a pyramid scheme is, and Primerica is not one of them. To clarify this issue we created the following chart to compare how Primerica ranks beside typical MLMs (multi-level marketing companies).

# Financial Freedom

| TYPICAL MLM | PRIMERICA |
| --- | --- |
| Privately owned | Public traded on NY Stock Exchange |
| Based in basement or home-office, if any | Thousands of professional offices |
| Sales based on internal consumption | Sales based on public consumption |
| Makes money off recruits (startup kit) | No income from signing recruits |
| Owned by a few founders | Real ownership available to all |
| Very few make any real money | 3,600+ people making $100,000 /yr or more |
| Mostly unregulated industries | Reps must be state/provincially licensed |
| Inflated prices for products/services | Competitive prices |
| Artificial/fabricated demand | Stable/growing/long-term demand |
| Need to get in on "ground-floor" | 40+ years and only 3% market penetration |

**Note:** In the spirit of full disclosure, the authors have spoken at many of Primerica's field leaders' events. We have done so because we, like Primerica, have a mission of bringing financial literacy to the Middle Class. The authors have never been representatives of Primerica, have never received any money to promote the company, and have never owned any Primerica stock.

# If You Fail to Plan You are Planning to Fail

If you are committed to setting up a new business, you need some form of a plan. Because traditional business plans are very cumbersome and difficult for the average person, we have developed an extremely simplified business plan. If you photocopy and fill in the following charts, investing the time needed to obtain accurate information, your chances of success will dramatically increase. As you go through this process you will likely uncover potential challenges that must be addressed before launching your business. The point of the exercise is to eliminate as many surprises as possible and stack the odds in your favor. Although this plan is simple, it is still a very powerful method of communicating the viability of a business idea to a potential partner, investor or lender.

# Financial Freedom

This chart will help you organize your thoughts in a brief written overview of your business idea.

| Achieving Financial Freedom Business Plan<br>Business Idea Overview |
| --- |
| What does this business entail? |
| What is the business structure (Sole proprietorship, partnership, limited company?) |
| Who are the business owners? |
| What products or services will be offered? |
| What experience, skills and knowledge does the business owner team have in this industry? |
| Who are the prospective clients? |
| A)How many clients can I serve in a single day?<br>B) How many clients could I serve if I were able to duplicate myself? |
| What is the projected future demand? |
| Who is your competition? |
| What are your competitive strengths versus your competitors? |
| What are the risks? How will you overcome them? |
| How much of the startup capital are the owners committing to? |
| What collateral is available to secure business debt? |
| What is the investors' expected Return on Investment? |

# Financial Freedom

| Achieving Financial Freedom Business Plan. | |
|---|---|
| **Projected Upfront Costs:** | **Amount** |
| Business idea research | |
| Cost to develop a prototype | |
| Business registration/Cost of incorporation | |
| Permits/Licenses | |
| Patent/Copyright registration | |
| Skills/Knowledge upgrading | |
| Professional memberships | |
| Insurance | |
| Marketing Materials:<br>• Business cards<br>• Letterhead<br>• Brochures<br>• Flyers<br>• Videos<br>• Website<br>• Signage<br>• Paid Advertising<br>• Other | |
| Business Supplies | |
| Raw goods and materials | |
| Purchase/rent: equipment/ tools/ machines | |
| Professional Fees:<br>• Bookkeeper/Accountant<br>• Lawyer<br>• Consultant | |
| **Total Projected Up-Front Costs** | |

| Projected Monthly Costs: | Amount |
|---|---|
| Rentals: Office/Storage/Warehouse/Retail Shop/ Furniture | |
| Vehicles | |
| Utilities: electricity/water/natural gas/oil_ | |
| Parking | |
| Janitorial/Cleaning fees | |
| Financial Charges:<br><br>• Banking & Credit card merchant fees<br>• Interest expenses<br>• Bad Debts | |
| Refunds or Returned product | |
| Telephone - Land lines & mobile phones | |
| Internet | |
| Advertising | |
| Cost to purchase or produce goods for (re)sale | |
| Travel, including accommodations & meals | |
| Postage/courier | |
| Sales commissions | |
| Employee wages & benefits | |
| Insurance | |
| Taxes: property, municipal, state/provincial | |

# Financial Freedom

| Projected Monthly Costs: | Amount |
|---|---|
| **Total Projected Monthly Costs** | |

| Projected Sales for Month of: | |
|---|---|
| **Service or Product:** | **Amount** |
| Service 1 | |
| Service 2 | |
| Service 3 | |
| Product 1 | |
| Product 2 | |
| Product 3 | |
| **Total Projected Sales for month:** | |

| Financial Viability Assessment | |
|---|---|
| **Category** | **Amount** |
| Available Start-up capital | |
| Total projected upfront costs | |
| Total projected monthly costs x 12 | |
| Total forecast sales for first year | |
| **Net projected surplus or shortfall** | |

Now that you have completed The **Achieving Financial Freedom** Business Plan and have confirmed the viability of the idea, you can now proceed on your own, or you can approach an investor or lender for financing.

## Avoid Failure

New businesses are more likely to fail when:

- The owner loses track of his or her goal.
- The owner plunges in without first considering testing things on a small scale.
- Goods or services are under priced or overpriced.
- The entrepreneur fails to be personally effective at selling his or her brand/products/services.
- The entrepreneur underestimates how much time it will take to build a market.
- The entrepreneur forgets to set aside money for taxes.
- The business is under capitalized.
- The entrepreneur starts with too much capital and spends it recklessly.
- The entrepreneur does not have sufficient knowledge about the chosen business sector.
- The entrepreneur does not have a clear plan for a repaying schedule for the money borrowed to start the business.
- The entrepreneur does not anticipate setbacks and unexpected expenses.
- The entrepreneur bases too much of his business on credit.
- The entrepreneur extends too much credit to unproven clients.
- The entrepreneur fails to track key business numbers daily.
- The entrepreneur does not keep complete and accurate records.
- The entrepreneur uses business accounts for personal spending sprees.
- The entrepreneur disregards business cycles or the buying patterns of clients.
- The entrepreneur slows the intensity of expansion because of a few successes or setbacks.

## Know Your Numbers

If you don't set goals and measure your progress, it's impossible to gauge how well you are doing relative to your goal. Making $400,000 of income is different than $40,000. The higher your goal, the more you'll need to step up your game. Measuring performance dates back as early as the Hammurabi Code and, more recently, when Kaplan and Norton in 1992 introduced Key Performance Indicators (KPIs). KPI's simply identify the six to twelve critical benchmarks that measure the overall financial health of a business.

Consider someone feeling very sick and unaware of the cause. If they go to the emergency room or their family doctor, the first thing the doctor will do is assess the person's personal health KPIs: blood pressure,pulse rate, breathing rate, and temperature. The quick assessment of these four health indicators can rule out many causes and can fast track the physician to understanding how to help the patient.

# DID YOU KNOW

Key Performance Indicators must reflect the uniqueness of each business. The following example shows how senior executives at a multi-billion dollar airline can review fewer than a dozen numbers a day and still accurately assess the exact health of their business. The KPI elements are bolded in the list below. Remember: these issues relate specifically to an airline.

- **Money**: % of seats sold and the amount per seat;

- **Employee Engagement**: Surveys and the absence of strikes, work-to-rules;

- **Training/Development**: Ability to provide medical response in flight, dealing with "mystery flyers";

- **Responsibility**: Free flights for poor children and patients needing medical attention; new airplanes with a smaller carbon footprint;

- **Internal Processes**: The percentage of on-time departures and arrivals, lost or delayed baggage numbers, optimal baggage/cargo ratios;

- **Customer Satisfaction**: Retention and growth of frequent flyer program, and IATA Travel Ratings.

The point is to know your critical numbers AND to track them daily. You also need to know which daily disciplines and activities will drive each critical number. As your business and your team grow, you need to teach your people what the critical numbers are, and create friendly competitions and post the top performers on some sort of a "Leaders Board." Real winners thrive under this positive competitive environment. Make sure that you recognize and reward your leaders, because others will compete even harder to receive public accolades the next time.

> You don't have to be **great** to start,
> but you have to **start** to be great.
>
> Zig Ziglar

# Financial Freedom

## Achieve Financial Freedom

How to Get a Fast Start on Your Financial Freedom Dream:

1. Be coachable. Put your ego away and listen to the wisdom of others.
2. Find a coach. Ask questions; learn from their examples.
3. Plug into relevant training. Look for industry-specific workshops and online videos.
4. Re-connect with your Why and your dreams and goals daily.
5. Know your top 10 daily disciplines and do them. No exceptions.
6. Get out of your Comfort zone. Find things that challenge you, and do them anyway.
7. Get comfortable talking to everyone about your business.
8. Make it about them. Remember to focus on your client's and teammate's dreams, not just yours. Take care of them and they will take care of you.
9. Focus on "Productivity" not just "Activity."
10. Join or create a breakfast club or Mastermind group. Hold yourself and others accountable.
11. Know your numbers and compete with yourself and others to grow.
12. Stop making excuses about why it's not working. Be bold! Meet people and, as Nike says, "Just Do It"!

## Conclusion

Starting your own business is simultaneously the scariest and most fulfilling thing you will ever do. There are no guarantees of success, so you need to guard against being blindsided, and be prepared to survive at least the most predictable disasters. Excluding unforeseen circumstances, in our experience the reason most start-ups fail is attributable to deficiencies outlined in the first section of this book: people haven't sufficiently connected with their Why or their Dream; or they skipped too quickly through some of the critical steps, such as the 7Rs. Remember, you don't have to carry all the weight on your own. Join a local Accelerator or Incubator program. Challenges that seem overwhelming to you may be very manageable to people who have already been through your stage of development. Please don't let haste short-change your chances of success. Financial Freedom can be yours. Good Luck!

# Explode Your Business!

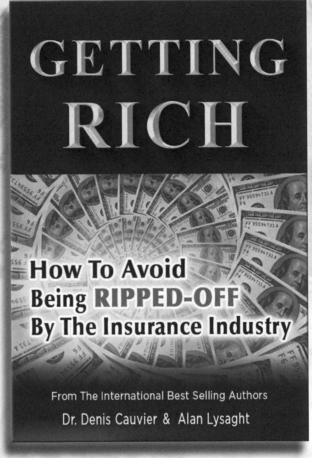

**GETTING RICH**

How To Avoid Being **RIPPED-OFF** By The Insurance Industry

From The International Best Selling Authors
Dr. Denis Cauvier & Alan Lysaght

*"This book will take your business to a whole new level."*

**Mario Arrizon, SNSD**

*"The most amazing book on life insurance I've ever seen!"*

**Rick Miller, Curt Joiner, SVPs**

To order:

# www.abcguys.com